Flight

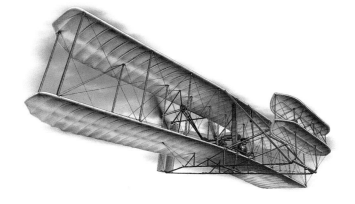

First published in Great Britain in 1995
by Macdonald Young Books Ltd
Campus 400, Maylands Avenue, Hemel Hempstead, Herts HP2 7EZ

Conceived and produced by Weldon Owen Pty Limited
43 Victoria Street, McMahons Point, NSW 2060, Australia
A member of the Weldon Owen Group of Companies
Sydney • San Francisco • London
Copyright © 1995 Weldon Owen Pty Limited

Publisher: Sheena Coupe
Managing Editor: Rosemary McDonald
Project Editor: Kathy Gerrard
Text Editor: Claire Craig
Editorial Assistant: Selena Quintrell Hand
Art Director: Sue Burk
Designer: Mark Nichols
Series Design Consultants: Alex Arthur, Arthur Brown
Assistant Designer: Angela Pelizzari
Picture Research Coordinator: Jenny Mills
Picture Research: Annette Crueger
Illustrations Research: Peter Barker
Production Director: Mick Bagnato
Production Coordinator: Simone Perryman

Text: Terry Gwynn-Jones

Illustrators: Christer Eriksson, Alan Ewart, Greg Gillespie, Mike Gorman,
Terry Hadler, Langdon G. Halls, David Kirshner, Mike Lamble, Alex Lavroff,
Kent Leech, Ulrich Lehmann, Oliver Rennert, John Richards, Trevor Ruth,
Steve Seymour, Ray Sim, Steve Trevaskis, Ross Watton/Garden Studio,
Rod Westblade

A catalogue record for this book is available from the British Library

ISBN 0-7500-1736 8

Manufactured by Mandarin Offset
Printed in China

A Weldon Owen Production

Flight

CONSULTING EDITOR

Donald Lopez

Senior Advisor Emeritus, National Air and Space Museum,
Smithsonian Institution, Washington D.C

MACDONALD YOUNG BOOKS

Contents

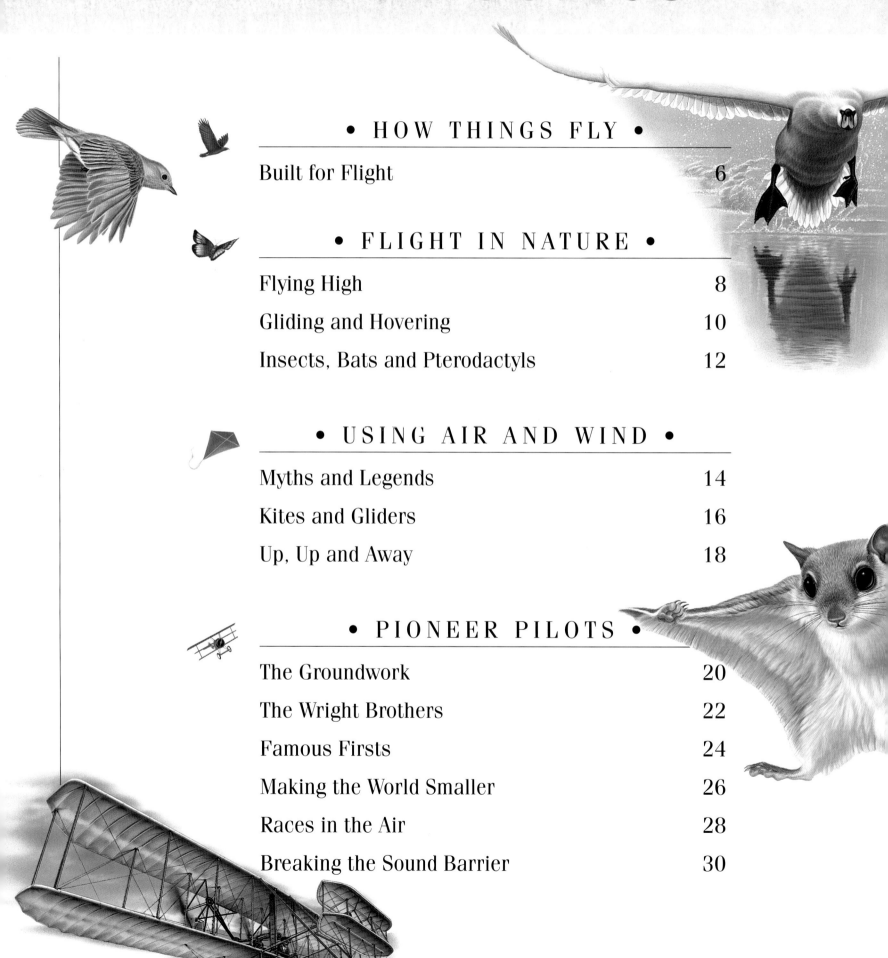

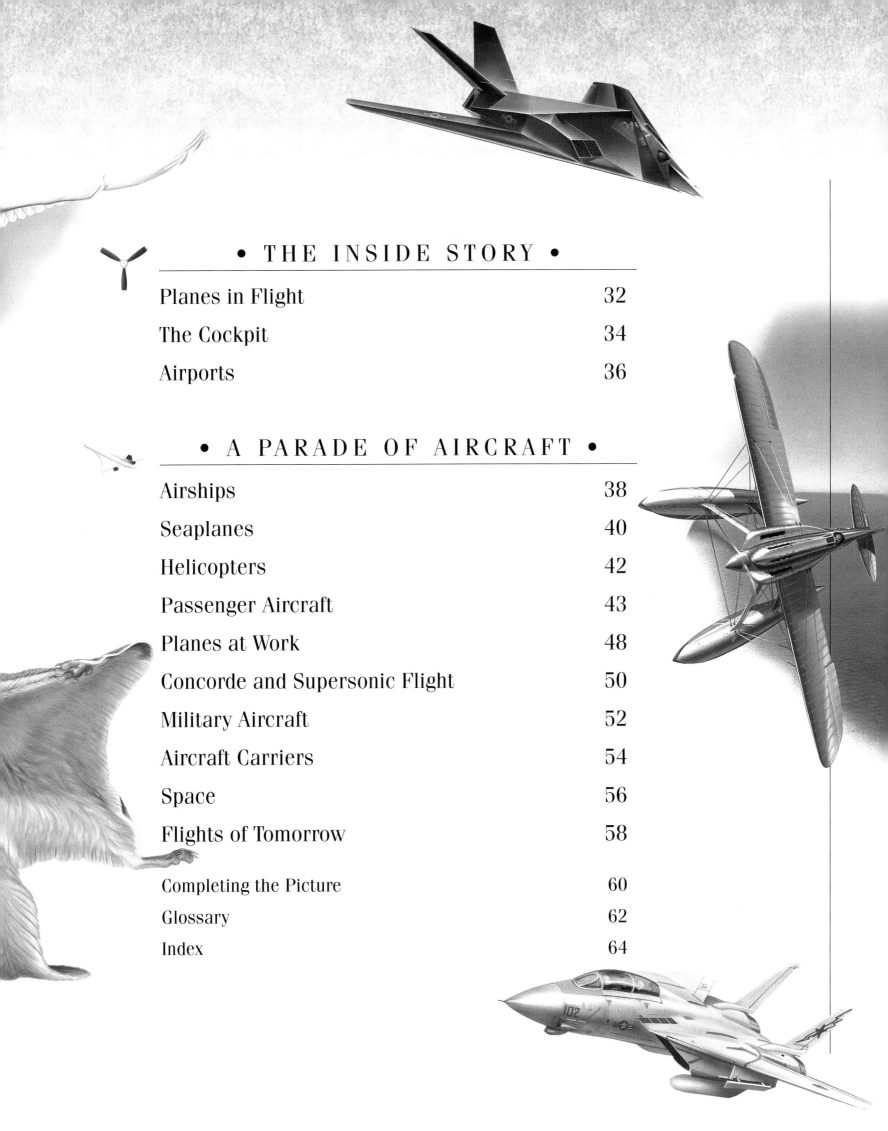

• THE INSIDE STORY •

• A PARADE OF AIRCRAFT •

Geese often fly in a V formation on a long flight. The bird in front does much of the work needed to fly through the air, and the other birds benefit from this. When the bird in front tires, another takes its place as leader. It is a little like walking in freshly fallen snow. This is hard work, but if you can walk in already made footprints, it is less difficult to forge your way through the heavy snow.

TAKE OFF
Swans are heavy birds. They need to run over the water for quite a long distance before they can build up enough speed to support their great weight in the air. For the same reason, aircraft that are laden with passengers or cargo also need a long runway to become airborne.

• HOW THINGS FLY •

Built for Flight

Have you ever watched birds in the sky and thought how easy it looks to fly? Centuries ago, people dreamed of joining birds in flight. Some went even further and flapped about, vainly, in wings made of feathers. But the human body is heavy and does not have the muscles needed for flight. The pioneers of aviation soon realised that before they could join the birds, they needed to understand how birds flew. They discovered that the wings of a bird are specially curved surfaces, called aerofoils. When air flows over a bird's wings, a difference in air pressure is produced above and below the wings. This difference in pressure creates a force called "lift", which can overcome the weight of a bird or a plane. This is called heavier-than-air flying, and gliders and aeroplanes also fly this way. Balloons and airships are lighter-than-air fliers. They are filled with hot air (which always rises) or gases, such as helium or hydrogen that are lighter than the air around them.

DID YOU KNOW?
Hydrofoils produce lift in water, just as aerofoils give lift in air. This fast boat has hydrofoils, which lift it up and enable the boat to skim along the surface of the water.

HEAVIER-THAN-AIR FLIERS
The wings of a swan and a giant Boeing 314 flying boat work in the same way. They produce the lift that is necessary to take off from the water.

ON THE WING
This cutaway shows the aerofoil of a bird's wing.

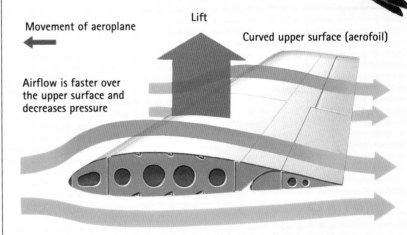

Movement of aeroplane

Lift

Curved upper surface (aerofoil)

Airflow is faster over the upper surface and decreases pressure

Airflow is slower over the lower surface and increases pressure

HOW AN AEROFOIL WORKS

This picture of an aeroplane wing moving through the air shows how its shape, or aerofoil, affects the airflow. The airflow passing over the wing's curved upper surface is faster than the airflow passing over the lower surface. This causes a difference in pressure, which lifts or sucks the wing upwards, as shown in the experiment on the left.

THE SECRET OF LIFT
Hold a sheet of paper as shown here. Blow hard over its upper surface and watch the paper lift up—just like an aeroplane's wing.

Flying High

Birds fly higher, farther and faster than any other flying animals. Many species can span entire oceans and continents on their migrations. Birds are also the only flying animals that regularly use the wind as a source of lift. A bird's wings are powered by two sets of muscles on the breast. In most birds, these muscles make up about one-third of their total weight. Muscle power moves the long, stiff flight feathers. Feathers at the wing tips, called primaries, propel the bird forward, while the rest of the wing generates the lift. The wings change shape as they beat up and down. They are broad and extended on the downstroke, but tucked in tight on the upstroke. Wing shape and how a bird lives are closely related. Long wings are more efficient than short wings, but much harder to flap. Birds with long wings are usually soaring birds. Short-winged birds have less stamina, but can build up speed very quickly.

WIDE WINGS
A spotted harrier eagle has wide wings and flies slowly over open country, looking for small reptiles, birds and mammals.

IN SLOW MOTION
The wingbeat of a European robin is a smooth alternation between the wings moving upwards (upstroke or recovery stroke) and the wings moving downwards (downstroke or powerstroke). It takes place in a cycle that is almost too fast to see. The process is broken into five stages (below) to show the details.

Flight control
The long feathers of the tail help to control the flight, especially steering and braking.

FEATHER CLOSE UP
Birds are the only animals that have feathers. An electron micrograph shows the intricate structure of a feather. It is held together by minute barbs and barbules like a Velcro fastener.

SPREADING OUT
The wings are high, fully spread and thrown forward. The feathers are overlapped and the feet are tucked against the body. The curled primary tips are like the angled blades of a propeller, and pull the bird forward.

TUCKING IN
The wings are tucked well into the body throughout the upstroke to reduce air resistance.

BEGINNING
At the start of the upstroke, the robin's feathers are separated. This reduces air resistance and the bird uses less energy.

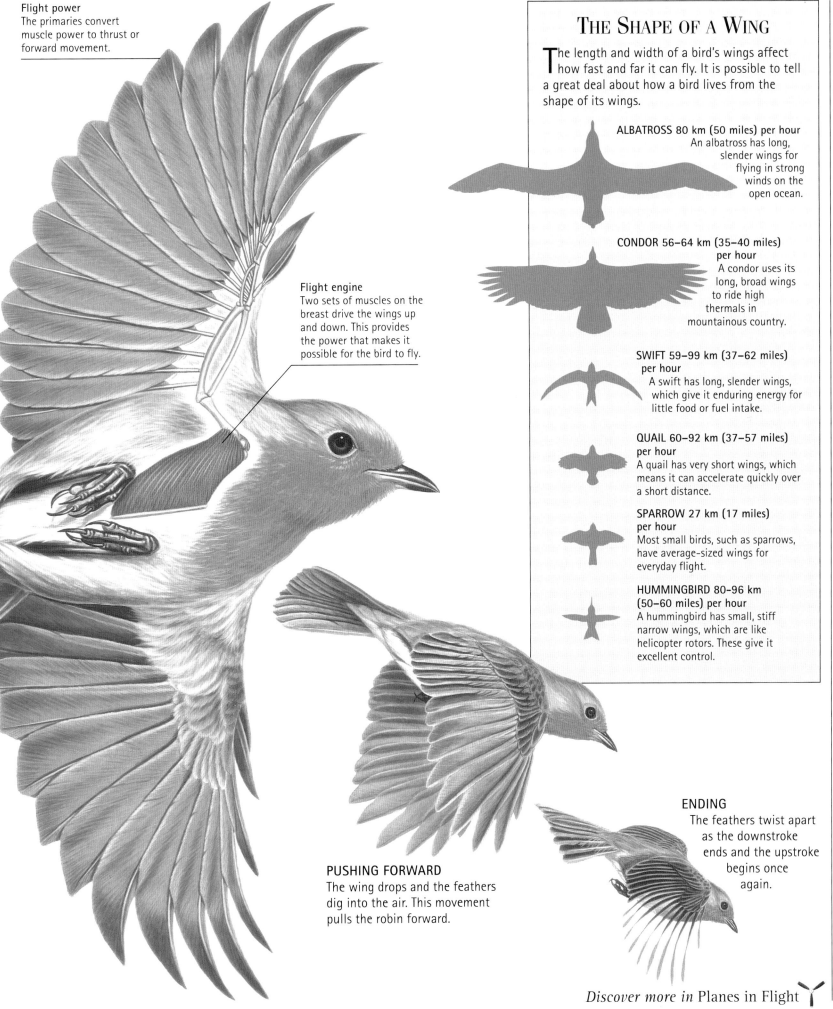

Flight power
The primaries convert muscle power to thrust or forward movement.

Flight engine
Two sets of muscles on the breast drive the wings up and down. This provides the power that makes it possible for the bird to fly.

THE SHAPE OF A WING

The length and width of a bird's wings affect how fast and far it can fly. It is possible to tell a great deal about how a bird lives from the shape of its wings.

ALBATROSS 80 km (50 miles) per hour
An albatross has long, slender wings for flying in strong winds on the open ocean.

CONDOR 56–64 km (35–40 miles) per hour
A condor uses its long, broad wings to ride high thermals in mountainous country.

SWIFT 59–99 km (37–62 miles) per hour
A swift has long, slender wings, which give it enduring energy for little food or fuel intake.

QUAIL 60–92 km (37–57 miles) per hour
A quail has very short wings, which means it can accelerate quickly over a short distance.

SPARROW 27 km (17 miles) per hour
Most small birds, such as sparrows, have average-sized wings for everyday flight.

HUMMINGBIRD 80–96 km (50–60 miles) per hour
A hummingbird has small, stiff narrow wings, which are like helicopter rotors. These give it excellent control.

PUSHING FORWARD
The wing drops and the feathers dig into the air. This movement pulls the robin forward.

ENDING
The feathers twist apart as the downstroke ends and the upstroke begins once again.

Discover more in Planes in Flight

9

SUSPENDED ABOVE
Hummingbirds feed mainly on nectar from flowers. This is a good source of energy and gives them plenty of fuel for their flights. They can fly in any direction or hover in midair, flapping their wings so fast it looks as if they are not flapping them at all.

• FLIGHT IN NATURE •

Gliding and Hovering

Some forest-dwelling animals can leap safely from one tree-branch to another. The southern flying squirrel glides on a furry membrane of skin. It can fly 100 m (328 ft) when there is no wind. But this is a very basic form of flight because the squirrel cannot fly for long and its control is very limited. True flight—for animals as well as aircraft—depends on keeping a constant flow of air over a wing's surface. Animals do this in two ways: they exploit the wind by soaring; or they rely on muscle power, through flapping wings, to maintain the airflow. Hovering is an extreme example of flapping. It gives the animal great control and manoeuvrability, but it also demands an enormous amount of power. A hummingbird hovers with seemingly little effort. In fact, the bird is working very hard. Imagine the enormous energy Olympic athletes use at the moment of their greatest effort. The hummingbird uses more than ten times this amount of energy to hover in the air.

TREE GLIDING
The southern flying squirrel uses the furry membrane between its outstretched limbs to glide from tree to tree. The membrane acts like a parachute and makes its fall gentle and safe. The squirrel also uses its long furry tail as a rudder to help it manoeuvre.

10

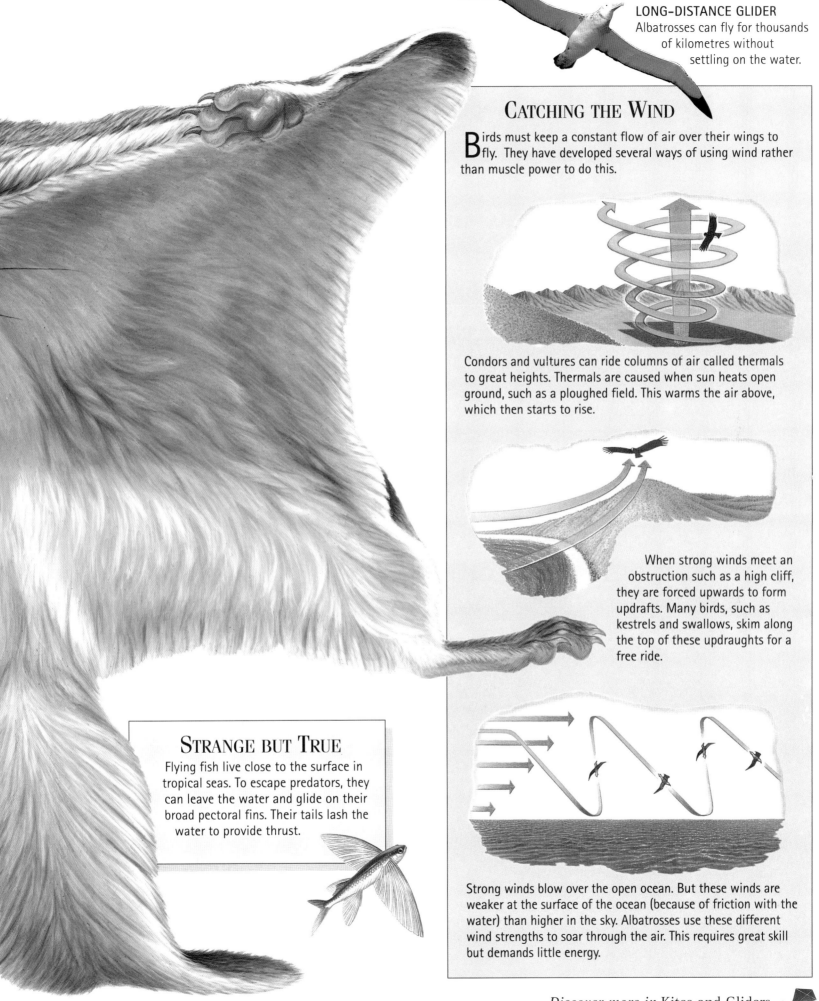

LONG-DISTANCE GLIDER
Albatrosses can fly for thousands of kilometres without settling on the water.

CATCHING THE WIND

Birds must keep a constant flow of air over their wings to fly. They have developed several ways of using wind rather than muscle power to do this.

Condors and vultures can ride columns of air called thermals to great heights. Thermals are caused when sun heats open ground, such as a ploughed field. This warms the air above, which then starts to rise.

When strong winds meet an obstruction such as a high cliff, they are forced upwards to form updrafts. Many birds, such as kestrels and swallows, skim along the top of these updraughts for a free ride.

STRANGE BUT TRUE

Flying fish live close to the surface in tropical seas. To escape predators, they can leave the water and glide on their broad pectoral fins. Their tails lash the water to provide thrust.

Strong winds blow over the open ocean. But these winds are weaker at the surface of the ocean (because of friction with the water) than higher in the sky. Albatrosses use these different wind strengths to soar through the air. This requires great skill but demands little energy.

Discover more in Kites and Gliders

11

Insects, Bats and Pterodactyls

Insects are the smallest of all flying animals. Their tiny muscles in tiny bodies are more efficient than large muscles in large bodies. Flying insects need less power than heavier animals such as bats and birds, and they are more manoeuvrable in the air. A housefly can somersault on touchdown to land upside down on a ceiling.

Insects, birds and bats are the only animals alive today capable of true flight. Bats fly using a membrane of skin, reinforced with muscle and tissue, which stretches between the arms and the legs (and sometimes the tail). Most bats are the size of a mouse and catch flying moths at night, but a few species weigh as much as 1.5 kg (3 lb) and feed on fruit. Long ago, at the time of the dinosaurs, another group of animals, called pterodactyls, also flew. They included the largest of all flying animals, the *Quetzalcoatlus*.

DID YOU KNOW?

Some insects, such as flies and mosquitoes, use their flight muscles to vibrate the sides of their body wall in and out. This makes the wings vibrate up and down together and creates the familiar buzzing or whining sound of an insect.

A CLOSER LOOK

A close-up of a dragonfly in flight shows some of the basic differences in the way insects, birds and bats are built for flight. Insects have two pairs of wings; birds and bats have only one. In birds and bats, the wings extend from the body, but in insects, they are entirely different structures.

CLOSER STILL

This electron micrograph shows where the wings of a dragonfly join to its body.

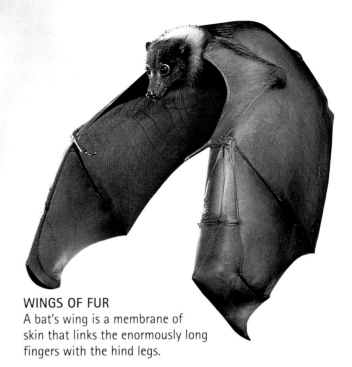

WINGS OF FUR
A bat's wing is a membrane of
skin that links the enormously long
fingers with the hind legs.

INSECTS' WING BEATS
The smaller the insect, the faster its wings
beat. This usually means its progress through
the air is also slower.

		SPEED PER HOUR	WING BEATS PER SECOND
	DRAGONFLY	24 km (15 miles)	35
	BUTTERFLY	22.4 km (14 miles)	10
	HOUSEFLY	14.4 km (9 miles)	170
	HONEYBEE	6.4 km (4 miles)	130
	MOSQUITO	1.6 km (1 mile)	600

PTERODACTYLS

The first machine to copy
the wing-flapping
technique of animal flight was
built as part of a study on the
flight of extinct pterodactyls.
A team of American scientists reconstructed a
pterodactyl called *Quetzalcoatlus northropi*, which lived
about 100 million years ago. Its wing span was around
6 m (19 ft) and it was equipped with a radio receiver, an
onboard computer "autopilot" and 13 tiny electric motors
to make the wings flap. In 1986, the model flew for three
minutes over Death Valley, California.

13

A SKY BIRD
The Garuda was a giant bird that carried the Indian god Vishnu across the sky. It is also the name of Indonesia's national airline, which uses the mythical bird for its logo.

• USING AIR AND WIND •

Myths and Legends

For thousands of years, people have told stories of wondrous beings that moved through the sky with the grace and ease of the birds. The ability to fly was seen as a sign of greatness and power. The gods and the heroes of many myths and legends were set apart from ordinary people because they could fly. In Greek mythology, Icarus and Daedalus flew on wings made of feathers, twine and flax; King Kaj Kaoos of Persia harnessed eagles to his throne; while Count Twardowski of Poland flew to the moon on the back of a rooster. Many people were inspired by visions of joining their heroes in the sky. They strapped wings to their arms and jumped off towers, high buildings and even out of balloons. Some did survive their dramatic falls. In 1507, Scotsman John Damian leapt from the walls of a castle with wings made of chicken feathers and broke only his thigh. He thought he would have been more successful if he had used the feathers of a bird that could really fly. The modern hero Superman can fly "faster than a speeding bullet". It seems our desire to believe in flying heroes continues.

A CHARIOT OF WINGS
Alexander the Great was said to have flown by harnessing four griffins, mythical winged-animals, to a basket. He placed meat on his spear and enticed them to fly after it.

A WINGED HORSE
According to Greek legend, Bellerophon the Valiant, son of the King of Corinth, captured a winged horse called Pegasus. He flew through the clouds to find and defeat in battle the triple-headed monster Chimera.

REACHING FOR THE SUN
In Greek mythology, Daedalus and his son Icarus used wax and feather wings to escape from the island of Crete. But Icarus flew too close to the sun and the wax on his wings melted. He fell into the Aegean Sea and drowned.

TOWER JUMPERS

Through the centuries, humans have tried to copy the birds. With elaborate wings made of feathers, they jumped from towers and flapped their arms desperately as they plummeted to the ground. They did not know that humans are too heavy and their muscles are not strong enough to fly like birds. The hearts of humans cannot pump blood fast enough to meet the demands of wing flapping, which even in a sparrow is 800 heartbeats a minute.

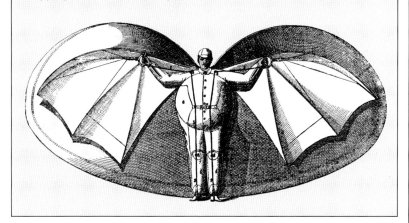

SKY BATTLE
In many legends the forces of both good and evil had the power to fly. Here, St Michael defends his island against a deadly dragon.

A TOUCH OF SPRING
The Egyptian goddess Queen Isis had wings like a falcon. Each year she flew over the Earth and brought spring to the land.

Discover more in The Groundwork

15

FORERUNNER OF FLIGHT
The Japanese used vibrantly coloured kites in religious ceremonies and for entertainment.

Wing shape
The main frame, called the spar, is shaped like a wing. It is stiff and curved to give the greatest lift.

HANG-GLIDING
A typical hang-glider flight begins on a high, windy ridge. Strapped into a harness, the pilot runs into the wind and is lifted by the sail (wing). The pilot holds the control bar and shifts his or her weight around to direct the hang-glider.

• USING AIR AND WIND •

Kites and Gliders

The kite is the ancestor of the aeroplane. The Chinese flew kites more than 2,000 years ago, and through the years they have been used to lift people high above battlefields on military observation, to collect weather information and to drop supplies. Kites inspired the English inventor George Cayley in his design of the world's first model glider. Pioneer fliers such as Englishman Percy Pilcher and German Otto Lilienthal used kite designs to develop the wings of their gliders. Lilienthal believed that aviators should learn to glide so they could really understand the air. The Wright brothers constructed their first glider in 1901 and this was based on a biplane kite they had built previously. Early gliders were launched from hills, but modern sailplanes are towed into the air by light planes. When they are released, they climb and soar in the sky, using thermals of hot air.

Control bar

MAORI FISHING KITE
The Maoris in New Zealand flew birdmen kites. Some had special significance and were used by "tohunga" (important men) to help them make big decisions.

16

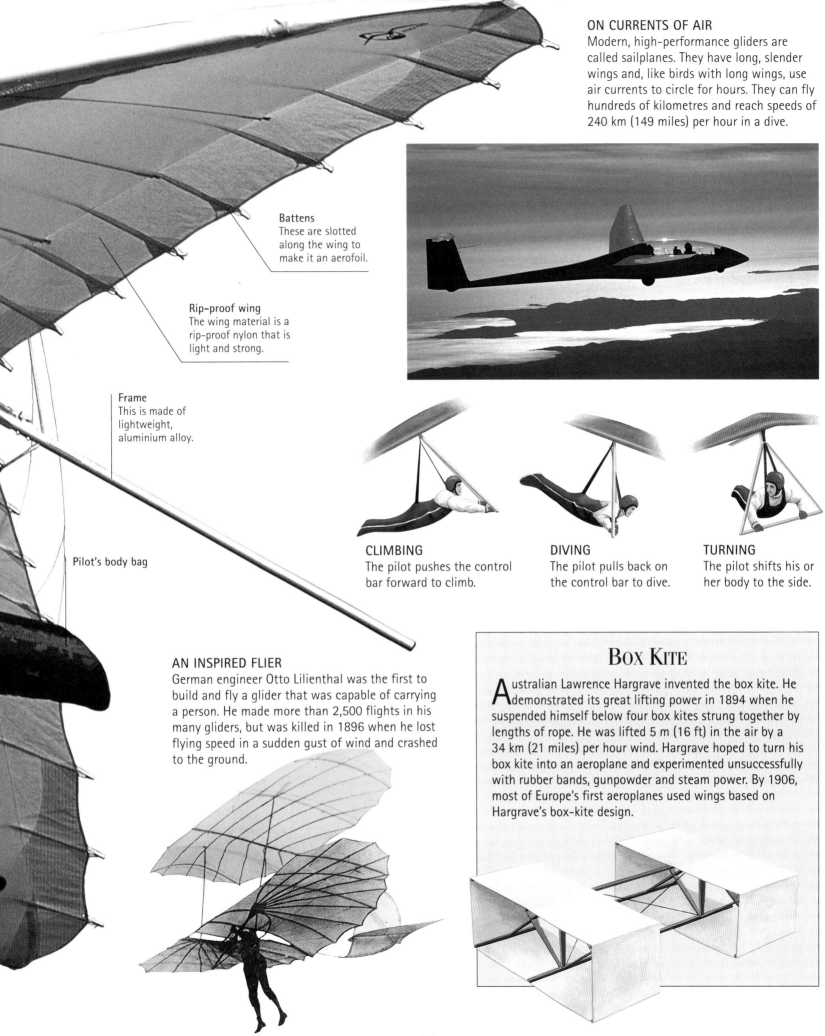

ON CURRENTS OF AIR

Modern, high-performance gliders are called sailplanes. They have long, slender wings and, like birds with long wings, use air currents to circle for hours. They can fly hundreds of kilometres and reach speeds of 240 km (149 miles) per hour in a dive.

Battens
These are slotted along the wing to make it an aerofoil.

Rip-proof wing
The wing material is a rip-proof nylon that is light and strong.

Frame
This is made of lightweight, aluminium alloy.

Pilot's body bag

CLIMBING
The pilot pushes the control bar forward to climb.

DIVING
The pilot pulls back on the control bar to dive.

TURNING
The pilot shifts his or her body to the side.

AN INSPIRED FLIER

German engineer Otto Lilienthal was the first to build and fly a glider that was capable of carrying a person. He made more than 2,500 flights in his many gliders, but was killed in 1896 when he lost flying speed in a sudden gust of wind and crashed to the ground.

BOX KITE

Australian Lawrence Hargrave invented the box kite. He demonstrated its great lifting power in 1894 when he suspended himself below four box kites strung together by lengths of rope. He was lifted 5 m (16 ft) in the air by a 34 km (21 miles) per hour wind. Hargrave hoped to turn his box kite into an aeroplane and experimented unsuccessfully with rubber bands, gunpowder and steam power. By 1906, most of Europe's first aeroplanes used wings based on Hargrave's box-kite design.

17

Up, Up and Away

People created many elaborate flying machines in their attempts to see the world from the sky. Frenchmen Joseph and Etienne Montgolfier built a balloon of paper and cloth that rose in the hot air above a fire. Their next balloon had passengers: a sheep, a duck and a rooster. In 1783, before an astonished crowd in Paris, a Montgolfier balloon (below) carried two French noblemen into the skies and became the first successful flying craft. Hot-air and gas-filled balloons soon became popular. When Paris was surrounded by a Prussian army in 1870, the French smuggled people and mail out of the city in balloons. In 1897, three explorers vanished trying to reach the North Pole in a balloon. Fifty years later, scientists used balloons to study the Earth's upper atmosphere. Today, several groups of balloon enthusiasts are planning to fly nonstop around the world.

Burners
The pilot reaches up and pulls the trigger operating the burner blast valve. Two propane gas burners blast heat into the balloon.

Basket
Most baskets are woven of willow, because it is strong, light and flexible.

FULL OF HOT AIR
Hot-air ballooning is very popular and many balloonists operate joy flights for the public. A typical balloon is 18 m (59 ft) in diameter and holds 2,830 cubic m (99,956 cubic ft) of air. This is heated by two propane gas burners, each of which is powerful enough to heat 120 houses.

Envelope
This is made of 24 panels of polyurethane-coated, rip-proof nylon. It usually contains 1,000 sq m (10,760 sq ft) of fabric and 5 km (3 miles) of thread.

Parachute vent

Ripcord

BALLOON ADVENTURERS
In 1978, *Double Eagle*, an American, gas-filled balloon, crossed the Atlantic in six days. Fifteen years later, a hot-air balloon (below) crossed Australia in 40 hours and 23 minutes.

BARRAGE BALLOONS
Clusters of gas-filled balloons were used to defend cities during the Second World War. They were tied to the ground by steel cables and obstructed enemy bombers that tried to fly low over the cities.

HOW HOT AIR BALLOONS FLY

Balloons travel with the wind, so balloonists have little control over their direction. But they can control the height to which they rise. If they want the balloon to climb, they turn the burner on. This heats the air in the balloon and produces lift. If a balloonist wants to descend, air in the balloon is allowed to cool, or the ripcord is pulled. Hot air then escapes from the parachute vent and is replaced by cooler (heavier) air. When the balloon has landed, the vent is opened to deflate the balloon.

Discover more in Airships

The Groundwork

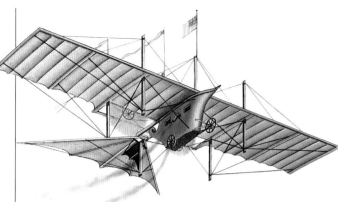

AERIAL STEAM CARRIAGE

In 1842, William Henson designed an aeroplane—the first flying invention to actually look like an aeroplane. It was to be powered by a steam engine, which turned two propellers. Although Henson managed only to build a model, his design had many of the features used in today's aeroplanes.

There are many stories of gallant people and the inspired flying contraptions they constructed. Most of the machines never flew, but these inventors and engineers did much of the groundwork for the aviators who were to follow. The development of the steam engine in the nineteenth century led to serious attempts to invent steam-powered aircraft. In 1874, Felix de Temple built a monoplane that managed a short, downhill hop. Clement Ader and Hiram Maxim both built machines that lifted them, briefly, off the ground. But these aircraft were difficult to control and their coal-fired steam engines were too heavy and not powerful enough for true flight. In 1896, Dr Samuel Langley launched an unpiloted aircraft with a steam-powered engine. It did manage to fly 1.2 km (1 mile), but then ran out of steam. Steam engines were soon replaced by light and powerful petrol engines. They made sustained flight a reality.

LANGLEY'S LUCKLESS VENTURE

American Samuel Langley made model aeroplanes powered by steam. They were so successful he built a full-sized version, called the *Aerodrome*, which had a petrol engine. Its first test flight was in 1903, when the piloted aircraft was launched from a catapult on the roof of a houseboat. But the launching mechanism failed, and *Aerodrome* plunged into the Potomac River.

ADER'S AEROPLANE

French engineer Clement Ader built his bat-like *Avion III* in 1897. It was larger than his previous invention *Eole*, but not as successful. In 1890, *Eole* managed a short hop and rose about 20 cm (8 in) into the air. *Avion III* never left the ground.

MAXIM'S MONSTER

This flying giant, a triple biplane with a wingspan of 31.5 m (103 ft), was built in 1894 by an American Hiram Maxim (the inventor of the machine gun). For a few seconds, its two steam engines lifted Maxim and his crew from its rail track.

DID YOU KNOW?

Artist Leonardo da Vinci (1452–1519) was also an engineer. He believed that ornithopters (wing-flapping aircraft) were the key to powered flight. He produced many plans for ornithopters, which ranged from strap-on wings to flying chariots.

THE SEARCH FOR AN ENGINE

In 1852, Henri Giffard built an airship, which was powered by the first aircraft engine—an extremely heavy, three-horsepower, steam engine. Aviators searched for an alternative with more power and less weight and experimented with electric motors and engines powered by compressed air and coal gas. In the late 1800s, Otto Daimler invented the petrol engine. This finally provided the light and powerful engine needed for heavier-than-air aeroplanes. The Anzani petrol engine shown here was invented in 1909.

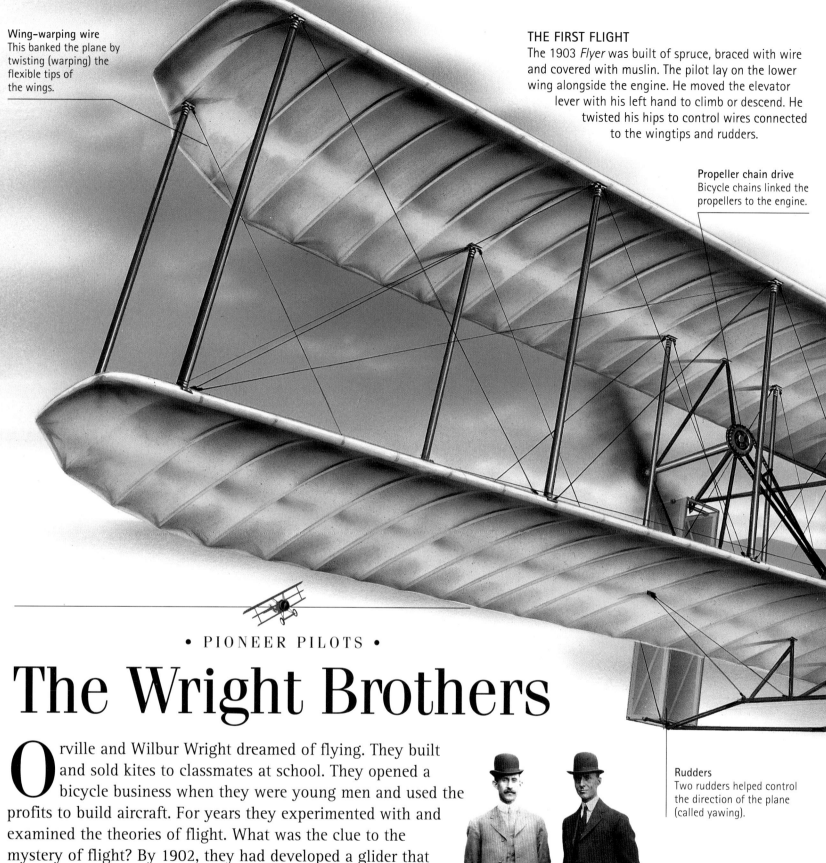

Wing-warping wire
This banked the plane by twisting (warping) the flexible tips of the wings.

THE FIRST FLIGHT
The 1903 *Flyer* was built of spruce, braced with wire and covered with muslin. The pilot lay on the lower wing alongside the engine. He moved the elevator lever with his left hand to climb or descend. He twisted his hips to control wires connected to the wingtips and rudders.

Propeller chain drive
Bicycle chains linked the propellers to the engine.

Rudders
Two rudders helped control the direction of the plane (called yawing).

• PIONEER PILOTS •

The Wright Brothers

Orville and Wilbur Wright dreamed of flying. They built and sold kites to classmates at school. They opened a bicycle business when they were young men and used the profits to build aircraft. For years they experimented with and examined the theories of flight. What was the clue to the mystery of flight? By 1902, they had developed a glider that could carry a person. It made more than 1,000 flights. Next, they designed and built a tiny 12-horsepower petrol engine and connected it by bicycle chains to a pair of propellers. It turned their glider into a powered aeroplane–the *Flyer*. In December 1903, Orville made the world's first powered flight from Kill Devil Hill, over Kitty Hawk beach in North Carolina. The first *Flyer* flew just four times, for a total of 98 seconds. Then, it was caught in a gust of wind and crashed into the sand–severely damaged.

DID YOU KNOW?
Wilbur (left) and Orville Wright tossed a coin to decide who would be the world's first pilot. Wilbur won, but he stalled and crashed into the sand. Orville succeeded where his brother had failed.

22

AHEAD OF ITS TIME
Orville Wright was part of a team that designed this streamlined, 1920 Dayton Wright monoplane racer. It had retractable landing gear, and extremely strong wings!

PROPELLER POWER

A propeller is a tiny wing that spins. As it rotates, air flows around the propeller blades and moves faster over the curved leading edge. This reduces the air pressure in front of the blade and pulls the aircraft forward. Many propellers allow pilots to adjust the blade angle for climbing, cruising and descending. This improves performance and keeps engine speed and fuel consumption low—like changing gears in a car. The propeller of the *Flyer* (shown on the right) was carved out of wood. Today, propellers are made of metal or fibreglass and carbon.

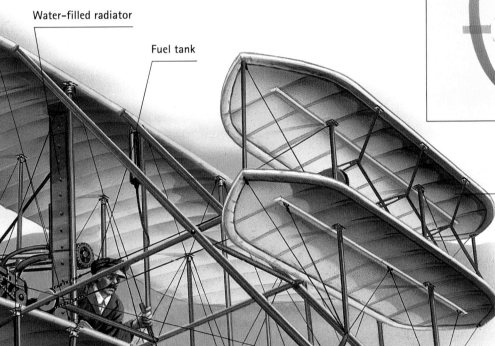

Water-filled radiator

Fuel tank

Biplane elevators
These tilted up or down to make the plane climb or descend.

Petrol-combustion engine
The 12-horsepower engine was mounted to the side to balance the pilot's weight.

Elevator lever

Skids for landing

THAT'S MY PLANE
The Wright brothers patented their aircraft in 1906 to stop others from copying their ideas. But aviators in Europe were already designing different kinds of aeroplanes.

A LATER PERSPECTIVE
Orville Wright's flight covered a distance of 51.5 m (170 ft), which included the take off and landing run. The whole flight could have taken place in the passenger area of this Boeing 747-400.

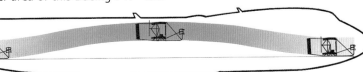

Discover more in Built for Flight

Famous Firsts

The progress of aviation has been marked by the achievement of many pioneers determined to dominate the skies. It all began in 1783 with the Montgolfier's hot-air balloon. In 1853, George Cayley created the first heavier-than-air aircraft. Fifty years later, the Wright brothers introduced powered flight and five years after, carried the first plane passenger. Louis Blériot flew across the English Channel in 1909 and proved that water was no longer an obstacle. Soon, time and technology would reduce flying times and the world would be encompassed by aeroplanes. In 1947, Chuck Yeager blasted through the sound barrier in his Bell X-1. Aviation sights were then set even higher, and in 1961, Russian Yuri Gagarin became the first person to fly in space. Six years later, the rocket-powered X-15A-2 reached a world-record speed of 7,254 km (4,497 miles) per hour—about 6.8 times the speed of sound.

WALKING ON THE MOON
Americans Neil Armstrong and Edwin "Buzz" Aldrin landed their lunar module *Eagle* on the moon on 21 July 1969. Their tentative steps were seen by millions of people all over the world.

PEDAL POWER
American cyclist Bryan Allen pedalled his *Gossamer Condor*, the first successful human-powered aircraft, around a 1.6 km (1 mile) figure-of-eight course in 1977. His aircraft cruised at 16 km (10 miles) per hour, had a wingspan of 29 m (95 ft) and weighed 32.7 kg (72 pounds). It was made of cardboard and aluminium tubing covered in plastic.

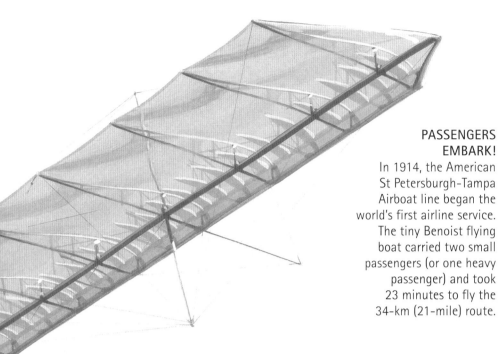

PASSENGERS EMBARK!

In 1914, the American St Petersburgh-Tampa Airboat line began the world's first airline service. The tiny Benoist flying boat carried two small passengers (or one heavy passenger) and took 23 minutes to fly the 34-km (21-mile) route.

WOMEN OF THE AIR

Women pilots were among those setting aviation firsts. In 1910, Baroness de Laroche from France became the first female pilot. Two years later, American Harriet Quimby flew the English Channel. Another famous American Amelia Earhart (above) was the first woman to fly the Atlantic in 1932. Other solo, long-distance pilots of the 1930s were Amy Johnson of England who flew 19,616 km (12,162 miles) to Australia; Australian Lores Bonney who flew 29,120 km (18,054 miles) to South Africa; and New Zealander Jean Batten whose array of firsts included crossing the South Atlantic. In 1953, American Jacqueline Cochran was the first woman to break the sound barrier.

JETTING ABOUT

In 1939, the German Heinkel He 178 became the world's first jet-powered aircraft. It could reach speeds of 700 km (434 miles) per hour. These aircraft had a great impact on aviation. All future designs for fighter planes in the United States and Europe were jet-propelled.

A FLYING MILESTONE

The sleek 1912 Deperdussin monocoque racer was the super plane of its day. Its single-shelled (monocoque) fuselage made it streamlined and fast. Flown by Frenchman Jules Vedrines, it was the first aircraft to exceed 161 km (100 miles) per hour.

Discover more in Breaking the Sound Barrier

CROSSING THE PACIFIC
In 1928, Australians Charles Kingsford-Smith and Charles Ulm made the first aerial crossing of the Pacific Ocean. They averaged 143 km (89 miles) per hour in their Fokker VII/3m *Southern Cross* on the 11,914 km (7,400 miles) flight. They stopped for fuel in Hawaii and Fiji.

THE WHITE CLIFFS OF DOVER
Louis Blériot flew from France to England in a monoplane, powered only by a 35-horsepower engine. He crash-landed on the cliffs of Dover after his great flight.

SPIRIT OF ST LOUIS
Lindbergh's plane, the Ryan NYP monoplane *Spirit of St Louis*, was built especially (in just two months) for his transatlantic flight. The 5,796-km (3,600-mile) flight from New York to Paris took 33 hours and 30 minutes. The cockpit of the plane was tucked behind a huge fuel tank and Lindbergh had to use a periscope to see in front of him.

• PIONEER PILOTS •

Making the World Smaller

As aeroplanes changed from rickety machines to planes that could cover huge distances, pilots dreamed of conquering large expanses of land and water. On 25 July 1909, Louis Blériot took nearly 37 minutes to become the first person to fly the 35 km (22 miles) across the English Channel. He battled wind gusts and a severely overheating engine to make a rushed downhill landing that shattered his propeller and landing gear. American Cal Rodgers survived five crashes to fly across the United States in 84 days in 1911. Ross and Keith Smith set an extraordinary record when they flew 18,396 km (11,426 miles) from England to Australia. Aviation dominated the headlines in 1927 when Charles Lindbergh flew the Atlantic, and a year later when Charles Ulm and Charles Kingsford-Smith conquered the Pacific. Jet travel eventually brought the continents less than a day's flight apart.

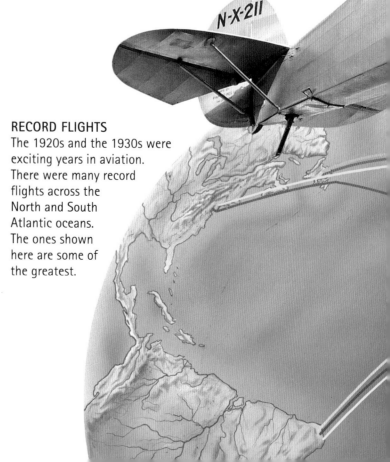

RECORD FLIGHTS
The 1920s and the 1930s were exciting years in aviation. There were many record flights across the North and South Atlantic oceans. The ones shown here are some of the greatest.

AROUND THE WORLD IN NINE DAYS
A long-distance aviation record was set in 1986 when Dick Rutan and Jeana Yeager flew their plane *Voyager* nonstop around the world in nine days.

ALTITUDE RECORD

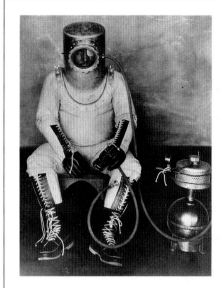

After flying around the world in 1934, American Wiley Post decided to break the world's altitude record. He designed the first spacesuit which, like a deep-sea diver's suit, allowed him to breathe and work at very high altitudes. In 1934, he reached a record 15,240 m (50,000 feet). He wore the suit when he made the first flights in jet streams—the high altitude winds used by today's airlines to increase their speed over the ground.

FLYING FAME
Charles Lindbergh began his flying career by carrying mail across the United States. He became the world's most famous pilot after his Atlantic crossing.

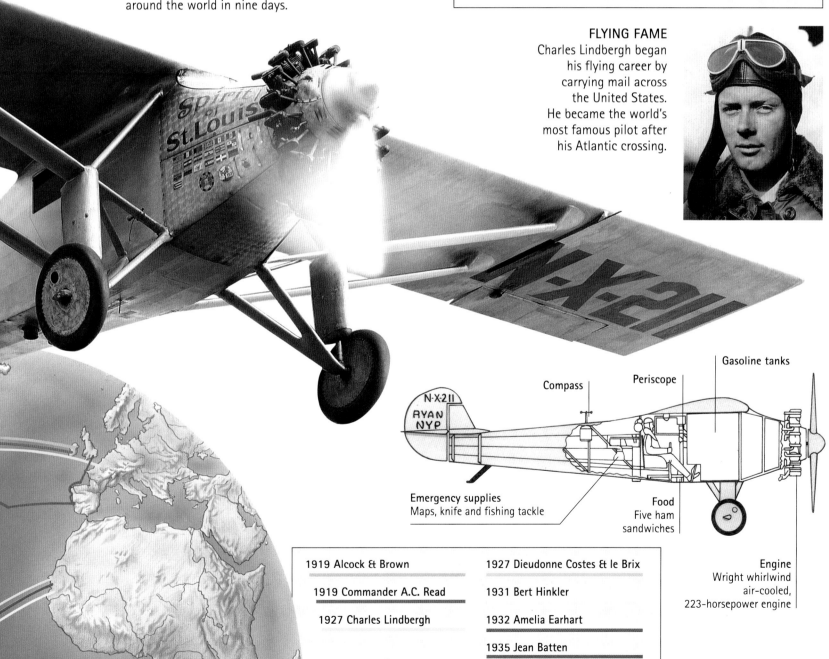

Compass

Periscope

Gasoline tanks

Emergency supplies
Maps, knife and fishing tackle

Food
Five ham
sandwiches

Engine
Wright whirlwind
air-cooled,
223-horsepower engine

1919 Alcock & Brown	1927 Dieudonne Costes & le Brix
1919 Commander A.C. Read	1931 Bert Hinkler
1927 Charles Lindbergh	1932 Amelia Earhart
	1935 Jean Batten

WEDDELL-WILLIAMS
The Weddell-Williams 44 racer won the American 1933 Thompson Trophy. It averaged 383 km (238 miles) per hour around a circuit marked by pylons. The racing planes of the 1930s relied on very powerful engines rather than streamlining for their speed.

• PIONEER PILOTS •

Races in the Air

People have always been competitive. The Wright brothers' wondrous flying machine introduced people to powered flight—a new way to gamble their lives for glory and the rich rewards of air racing. In 1909, American Glenn Curtiss won the world's first air race, the Gordon Bennett Cup, flying a rickety, open biplane at 76 km (47 miles) per hour. Three years later, aircrafts and speeds had improved dramatically and a Deperdussin monoplane flew at 199 km (123 miles) per hour to win the cup. In the 1930s, the National Air Races held in the United States attracted huge crowds, and pilots such as Roscoe Turner and Jimmy Doolittle became sporting heroes. Twenty-three women pilots, including Amelia Earhart, entered the first women's air race. The Schneider, Thompson and Bendix races continued to thrill the public and help refine aircraft design. Many pilots today recreate the excitement of the great air-racing days by flying specially built planes at events such as the Reno Air Races held in the United States.

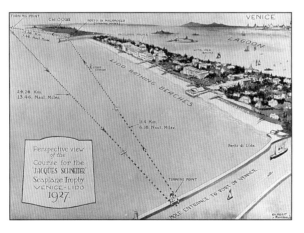

SCHNEIDER TROPHY
This race for seaplanes was held across open water. Racers flew seven times around a triangular 48-km (30-mile) course.

RACING FOR GLORY
The race is on as a British Supermarine S.5 leads an Italian Macchi M.52 around a pylon during the 1927 Schneider Trophy Race for seaplanes. Both machines were very streamlined, and this made them very fast. The winning S.5 averaged 454 km (282 miles) per hour.

28

AIR ACE
American Jimmy Doolittle was a top air racer. In 1925, he won the Schneider Trophy in a US Army seaplane. In 1931, he won the Bendix Trophy. He set a world record of 473 km (294 miles) per hour in 1932 when he won the Thompson Trophy.

BENDIX TROPHY
This trophy was awarded to the winner of a long-distance race across the United States, held between 1931 and 1949.

AERIAL SHOW-OFFS

After the First World War, many unemployed pilots earned a living as travelling showmen, giving joyflights at city shows and country fairs. Others worked for flying circuses and entertained the crowds with spectacular aerial tricks such as walking on wings, hanging upside down from the landing gear, transferring from one plane to another in flight, or playing tennis on the wings of a Curtiss Jenny biplane.

Breaking the Sound Barrier

FASTER THAN THE SPEED OF SOUND
As bullets were known to be supersonic, Bell aircraft shaped the fuselage of the X-1 experimental rocket plane like a .50 calibre bullet. The aircraft was powered by a rocket motor and launched from Boeing B-29 and B-50 bombers.

Imagine flying through the air and striking an invisible barrier. This happened to Spitfire and Mustang fighter pilots during the Second World War. At speeds of around 880 km (545 miles) per hour, their aircraft suddenly became difficult to control. The planes shook so violently that some even broke apart. These pilots were approaching the sound barrier, which many experts believed no aircraft could penetrate. Breaking through that barrier became an international challenge, and some pilots in the early jet fighters died in their attempts. But in 1947, Chuck Yeager blasted through the sound barrier in his specially designed Bell X-1, powered by a rocket engine. An American F-86 Sabre jet fighter then exceeded the speed of sound while in a dive. Today, aeroplanes such as Concorde and most military aircraft can easily fly faster than the speed of sound.

THE AREA RULE
This is a method of designing an aeroplane's shape to reduce drag. The red dashes on the F-102 above show the width of the middle fuselage before it was trimmed according to Area Rule calculations.

GLAMOROUS GLENNIS
At an altitude of 13,106 m (43,000 ft), Captain Charles "Chuck" Yeager flew through the sound barrier at 1,126 km (698 miles) per hour in *Glamorous Glennis*, named after his wife.

High-speed probe
This gathers information on air pressure during flight.

THE SOUND BARRIER
As it moves through the air, an aeroplane makes pressure waves that travel at the speed of sound. They radiate outwards like ripples from a stone dropped in a pond.

SUBSONIC: BELOW MACH 1
The pressure waves radiate in front of as well as behind the aeroplane.

Horizontal stabiliser
This moves to help control or stabilise the aircraft as it nears the sound barrier.

Rocket-engine plumes
The engine is a 2,722 kg (6,000 lb) thrust rocket, powered by liquid oxygen and ethyl alcohol.

Cockpit
This is pressurised and has room for one pilot.

SPEEDING THROUGH AIR
A Machmeter gives the speed of air as a percentage of the speed of sound, which varies with temperature. At 12,192 m (40,000 ft), where it is very cold, Mach 1.0 is 1,060 km (657 miles) per hour.

Wings
The wings are short and very thin to reduce drag at high speed.

DID YOU KNOW?
A thunderclap, rifle shot and whip-crack are tiny sonic booms. Like the boom of a supersonic aeroplane, they are created by shock waves—sudden increases in air pressure.

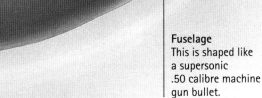

Fuselage
This is shaped like a supersonic .50 calibre machine gun bullet.

TEST PILOTS
Test flying requires skill and daring—pilots call it "the right stuff". Each new aircraft, whether it is the latest glider, jumbo jet, military fighter or space shuttle, must be tested in flight to check that it is safe and reliable. Test pilots push their machines through every imaginable flight manoeuvre until they are satisfied that there are no problems with the aircraft. This dangerous task has now been made easier by supercomputers that can simulate the flight performance of new designs before the actual planes are ever flown.

TRANSONIC: AT MACH 1
The aeroplane catches up with its own pressure waves, which build up into a shock wave.

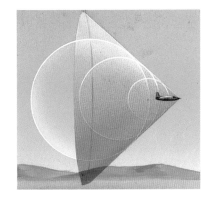

SUPERSONIC: ABOVE MACH 1
The shock waves form a cone. This causes a sonic boom when it hits the ground.

Planes in Flight

The invisible force that makes heavier-than-air aircraft fly is the flow of air around an aeroplane's wings. The differences in pressure above and below the wings combine to "lift" the aeroplane. "Lift" is one of the four forces that act upon a plane in flight and it overcomes the plane's "weight". The "thrust", or forward movement of the plane is produced by the engine and this opposes "drag", the natural resistance of the aeroplane to forward motion through the air. But an aeroplane also needs to be stable so that it can fly smoothly and safely. Its tailplanes and the dihedral shape of its wings (which means the wings are angled upwards slightly from the fuselage) make the plane stable in the same way the tail of a kite makes it steady. The wings and tailplanes are also equipped with movable control surfaces called ailerons, elevators and rudders. These alter the airflow over the wings and tailplanes, and the pilot uses them to change the aeroplane's direction and height.

Vertical tailplane (tailfin)

Horizontal tailplane

Control rods
These link the pilot's controls to the elevators and rudder.

Left aileron down

PITCHING
When the elevators are up, the aeroplane's nose is raised above the horizon and the aeroplane climbs. The rudder and ailerons are in a neutral position. When the aeroplane descends, the elevators are down. This up or down movement of the nose is called "pitching".

Elevators up

BANKING (ROLLING)
The left aileron is down and the right aileron is up, which makes the aeroplane bank to the right. The elevators and rudder are in a neutral position. This movement of the wings is called "rolling".

Right aileron up

ANGLE OF ATTACK
This is the angle at which the wing meets the airstream. As an aeroplane slows down, this angle must be increased to produce enough lift to equal its weight. When the angle reaches 14 degrees, the wing loses lift (called stalling) and the aeroplane descends.

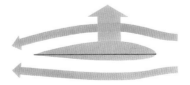

LOW ANGLE
At high speed, the wing needs only a low angle of attack (about 4 degrees) to produce enough lift.

HIGH ANGLE
At low speed, a much higher angle of attack is needed to produce the same amount of lift.

STALL ANGLE
At about 14 degrees angle of attack, the airstream over the wings becomes turbulent. The plane stalls and loses height.

Fuselage
The body of the aeroplane contains the cockpit and the engine. It is streamlined to minimise the drag caused by wind resistance.

Control column
This moves backwards and forwards to operate the elevators, and from side to side to operate the ailerons.

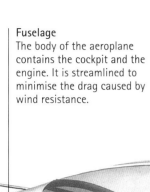

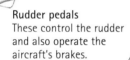

Rudder pedals
These control the rudder and also operate the aircraft's brakes.

DID YOU KNOW?
As an aeroplane flies higher, the pressure of the air outside decreases. The changes in pressure as an aeroplane climbs or descends can make your ears "pop". People with bad colds can experience painfully blocked ear drums.

Propeller
This has rotating blades, shaped like aerofoils, which convert the engine power into forward thrust.

THE CONTROL SURFACES
Ailerons, elevators and the rudder are operated by the control column and rudder pedals in the cockpit. They are used to make the aeroplane climb or descend, roll, turn or simply fly straight and level, as shown.

Rudder right

TURNING (YAWING)
The left aileron is slightly down, the right aileron is slightly up. The rudder is moved to the right, which helps to push the aeroplane's nose sideways into a gentle right turn. This sideways movement of the nose is called "yawing".

WING FLAPS
When birds land, they spread their feathers and change wing shape to touch down slowly. Aeroplane pilots do the same thing by lowering sections of the front and rear edges of the wing, called flaps and slats. These devices produce extra lift and help big jets to land and take off at slow speeds.

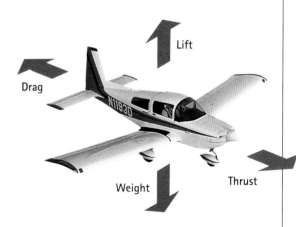

Lift

Drag

Weight

Thrust

When an aeroplane is in straight and level flight at a steady airspeed, the four forces are in equilibrium (balanced). This means that lift is equal and opposite to weight, and thrust is equal and opposite to drag.

Discover more in Airports

The Cockpit

The cockpit is the nerve centre of the aeroplane. It is crammed with controls, instruments and computers: some Boeing 747 cockpits contain 971 instruments and controls. Orville Wright had none of these devices. He had to lie on the lower wing of the plane and look at the horizon to judge the plane's position in flight. Pioneer pilots navigated by comparing features on the ground with those on their maps. Pilots today do not even have to see the ground. They use navigation systems that are linked to satellites, while the computer-controlled autopilot flies the aeroplane far more accurately than a human ever can. The latest instrument panels have television, radar and multi-function displays that give pilots the information they need to fly their planes safely.

HAND THROTTLE
This cluster of throttle levers operates the eight engines of a giant B-52 bomber.

A PILOT'S PERSPECTIVE
The Spitfire fighter was an important player in the air battles of the Second World War. The instruments and controls shown in this Spitfire cockpit are very similar to those found in small aeroplanes today.

FLIGHT SIMULATORS

Jet airliners are very expensive to fly, so machines called simulators are used to train pilots and to practise emergency drills. These machines are built to resemble the cockpit of an airliner. They have all the instruments and controls of a real plane. To make the simulator even more lifelike, moving pictures of the sky and ground are projected onto the windscreen—just like a giant video game.

BOEING 747
The flight crew of a modern airliner sits in a spacious cockpit using sophisticated computers and instruments that are large and easy to read.

NAVIGATIONAL DISPLAY
This display shows the aeroplane's position on a radar picture of the ground below. It also gives the aeroplane's speed, fuel flow, and the time and distance to the next position along the air route.

PRIMARY FLIGHT DISPLAY
In modern aeroplanes, all the instruments needed for "blind" flying are combined in this single display. It has replaced the cluttered flight instrument panel that was used in aeroplanes such as the Spitfire.

Airports

The first commercial airports were built in the 1920s. They usually consisted of a large grass field with a few small buildings, a hangar and a rotating searchlight beacon to help pilots find the airport in bad weather. Airports today are miniature cities, surrounded by a web of taxiways and runways that can be more than 4,000 m (13,120 ft) long. The busiest airport in the world is O'Hare Airport in Chicago—more than 2,000 aeroplanes land and take off every day. Huge numbers of passengers and large amounts of baggage pass through airports. When passengers first began travelling by air, they were weighed along with their luggage! The ground staff at airports look after the equipment needed to keep the aeroplanes flying safely. Movement of planes through an airport is regulated by air traffic controllers, who watch and use radar to monitor the planes' flight path.

NETWORKING
To keep aeroplane traffic flowing, busy airports such as San Francisco International Airport need a network of runways, taxiways and parking bays.

Stacking
Aircraft circle over a radio beacon as they await their turn to land.

CONTROL TOWER
The Control Tower provides a bird's-eye view of the airport and the surrounding sky. Its staff control the movement of all aeroplanes on the ground and in the air near the airport.

Outer marker
Shows that the aeroplane is 8 km (5 miles) from touchdown on final approach.

Middle marker
Marks the midway point of the final approach.

INSTRUMENT LANDING SYSTEM

In bad weather, pilots use the Instrument Landing System (ILS) to land safely. Two narrow radio beams are transmitted from the touchdown point on the runway. One is called the Glide-slope, the other is called the Localiser. If pilots follow the position of these two beams on an instrument in the cockpit, they can approach the runway and land the plane without seeing the runway until the final moment.

Glide-slope beam
Shows that the aeroplane is descending to the runway at the right angle.

Localiser beam
Shows that the aeroplane is properly in line with the runway.

Inner marker
At this point, close to touchdown, pilots should be able to see the runway.

RUSH HOUR
Airport staff rush around this 375-passenger Airbus at the terminal. In just 90 minutes, the airliner must be unloaded, cleaned, restocked with food and drinks, refuelled and boarded by new passengers.

DID YOU KNOW?
During take off and landing, the tyres of large aeroplanes speed across the ground. Friction with the ground can make them hot enough to catch fire. To avoid this, the tyres are filled with nitrogen, which does not burn, rather than air.

Toilet-waste truck
Removes waste from the aircraft toilets.

Cleaning service truck
This carries the cleaners and their equipment and takes away rubbish from the previous flight.

Mobile stairs
These give ground staff access to the cabin.

Fuel-transfer vehicle
This pumps aviation fuel from underground tanks into the aircraft tanks.

Conveyor
A moving belt carries late and awkwardly shaped baggage into the aircraft hold.

Aerobridge
A passenger walkway links the aircraft with the terminal.

Tractor and dollies
These bring passenger baggage to and from the terminal.

Water truck
This fills the aircraft's water tanks.

Hi-loaders
These platforms rise to load heavy containers.

Tow tractor
This pushes the aircraft from the terminal to the taxi area.

Catering truck
This stocks the aircraft with the in-flight meals and drinks.

Ground power unit

37

Airships

The first airship was a sausage-shaped balloon. It was built in 1852 by French engineer Henri Giffard, who fitted his new aircraft with a small steam engine and a rudder for steering. It flew 27 km (17 miles), but did not have enough power to fly against the wind. In 1900, Count Ferdinand von Zeppelin from Germany built the first rigid airship. It was longer than a football field and had a lightweight framework that contained huge gas bags or cells, each of which was filled with hydrogen—a highly inflammable gas. Between 1910 and 1913, Zeppelin airships carried more than 30,000 passengers on sightseeing flights over Germany. They were also used to bomb London in night raids during the First World War. The luxurious *Graf Zeppelin* and the *Hindenburg*, the largest rigid airship, carried thousands of passengers across the Atlantic between the two world wars. In 1937, however, the world was stunned when the *Hindenburg* exploded. The airship era came to an abrupt and tragic end.

A DRAMATIC END
The *Hindenburg* approached its mooring mast at Lakehurst, New Jersey, in the United States. Suddenly, flames and smoke billowed into the sky—the airship had exploded! Amazingly, 62 of the 97 people on board escaped from the blazing airship.

TRAVELLING IN STYLE
The *Graf Zeppelin* was the world's most successful airship. It was powered by five engines and had a top speed of 128 km (79 miles) per hour.

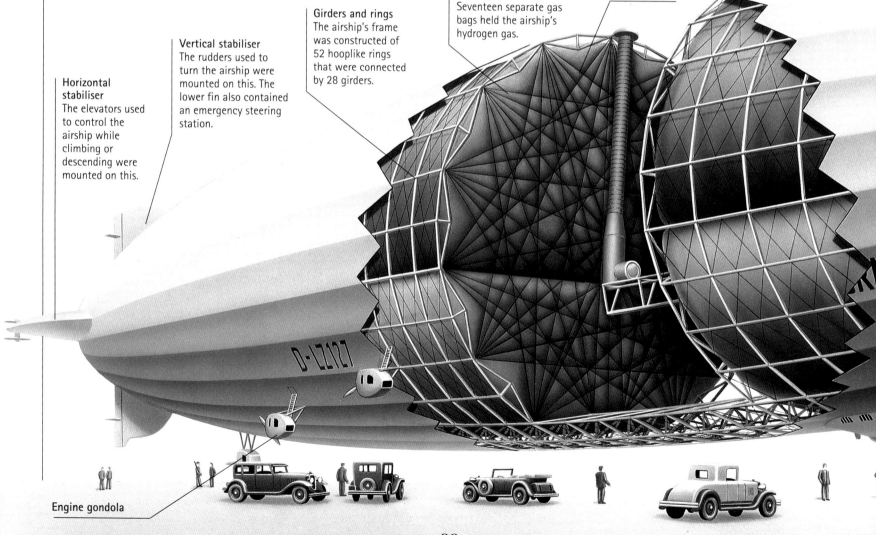

Horizontal stabiliser
The elevators used to control the airship while climbing or descending were mounted on this.

Vertical stabiliser
The rudders used to turn the airship were mounted on this. The lower fin also contained an emergency steering station.

Girders and rings
The airship's frame was constructed of 52 hooplike rings that were connected by 28 girders.

Gas bags
Seventeen separate gas bags held the airship's hydrogen gas.

Bracing wire

D-LZ127

Engine gondola

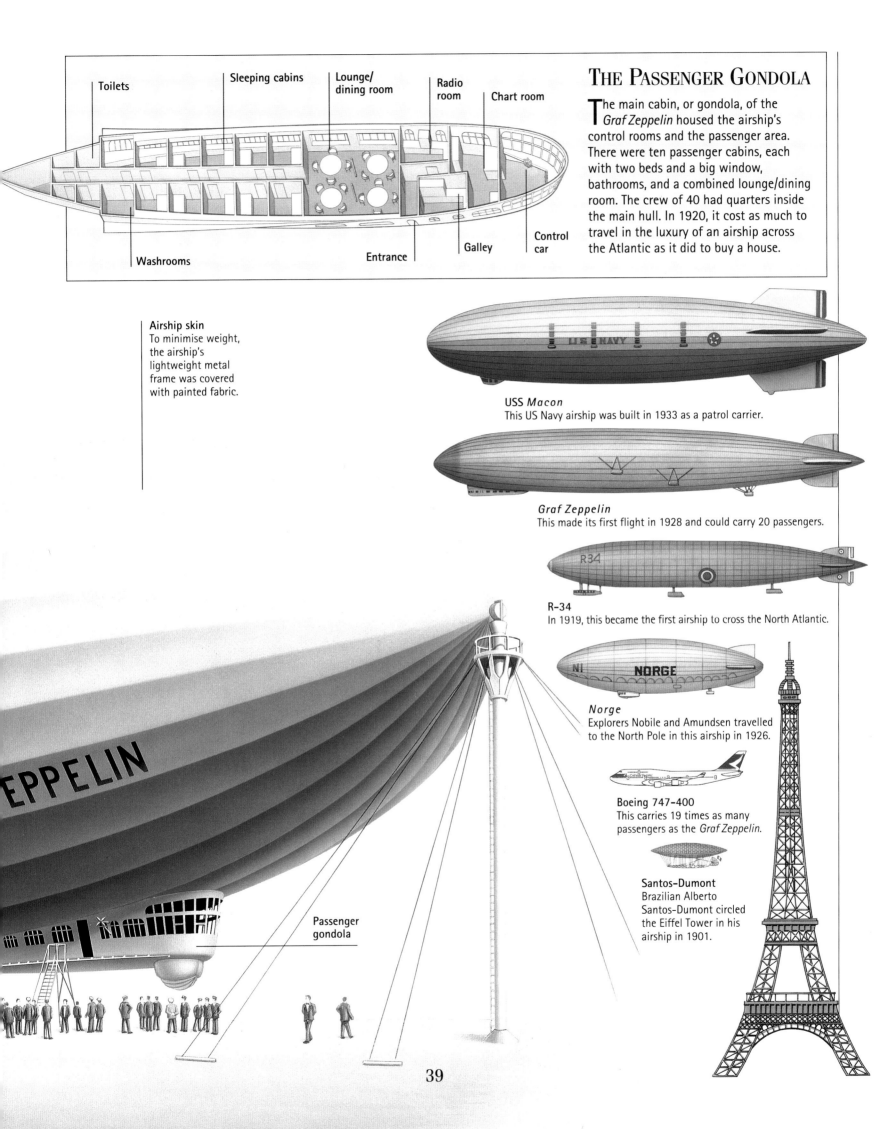

THE PASSENGER GONDOLA

The main cabin, or gondola, of the *Graf Zeppelin* housed the airship's control rooms and the passenger area. There were ten passenger cabins, each with two beds and a big window, bathrooms, and a combined lounge/dining room. The crew of 40 had quarters inside the main hull. In 1920, it cost as much to travel in the luxury of an airship across the Atlantic as it did to buy a house.

Toilets

Sleeping cabins

Lounge/ dining room

Radio room

Chart room

Washrooms

Entrance

Galley

Control car

Airship skin
To minimise weight, the airship's lightweight metal frame was covered with painted fabric.

US NAVY

USS *Macon*
This US Navy airship was built in 1933 as a patrol carrier.

Graf Zeppelin
This made its first flight in 1928 and could carry 20 passengers.

R34

R-34
In 1919, this became the first airship to cross the North Atlantic.

N1   NORGE

Norge
Explorers Nobile and Amundsen travelled to the North Pole in this airship in 1926.

Boeing 747-400
This carries 19 times as many passengers as the *Graf Zeppelin*.

Santos-Dumont
Brazilian Alberto Santos-Dumont circled the Eiffel Tower in his airship in 1901.

EPPELIN

Passenger gondola

Seaplanes

Pan American Airways called their flying boats Clippers after the fast sailing ships that crossed the oceans of the world a century earlier.

TRANSPACIFIC

T he 1930s was the age of the seaplane. People believed these aircraft were a safe way to cross stretches of water during a time when aircraft engines were thought to be unreliable. The luxurious flying boats, designed to compete with ocean liners, introduced people all over the world to the exotic reality of long-distance air travel between continents. Many airlines were now able to extend their services beyond Europe and North America. Pan American's Clipper flying boats provided the first passenger services across the Atlantic and Pacific. The Boeing 314 Clipper was the largest aeroplane of its day. It could carry 74 passengers and a crew of eight, and had 40 sleeping berths. Some flying boats were used to patrol the oceans for submarines during the Second World War. But the war also helped to bring about the end of the great flying boats. Land aircraft had improved enormously and airfields had been built all over the world.

Lounging and dining
At meal times the lounge became a restaurant where diners were served by waiters.

Engines
600 hp Wright double-cyclone engines.

Wing walkway
The engineer could walk along here to make minor repairs during the flight.

Radio operators

PASSENGER COMFORT
The enormous Boeing 314 had four massive engines and could cruise at a speed of 280 km (174 miles) per hour. It could also fly 5,600 km (3,472 miles) without refuelling.

Anchor
A ship's anchor was used when a mooring dock was not available.

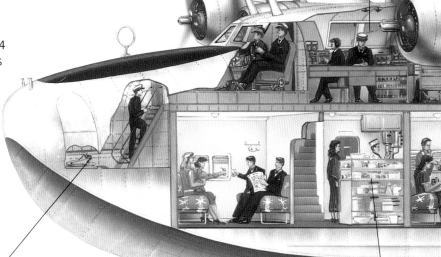

Galley
Meals were prepared and cooked on board. On modern airliners, food is reheated.

Sponsons
These stabilisers balanced the aircraft on the water and were used to hold fuel.

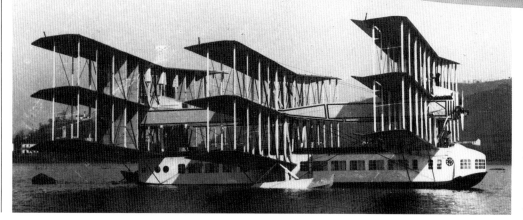

AN AVIATION FAILURE
This Italian flying boat, a 9-winged Caproni Noviplano, was designed to carry 100 passengers. Instead, it crashed on its first test flight in 1921.

Passenger Aircraft

Today, people travel for great distances across the world in airliners. The Boeing 747-400 can carry 400 passengers nonstop across the Pacific Ocean. The first airliner, however, was a tiny flying boat, with room for one passenger only. In 1914, it began flying between St Petersburg and Tampa, Florida—a flight time of 23 minutes. In the early 1920s, First World War bombers were converted to carry passengers, but these planes were soon replaced by specially designed passenger biplanes, and monoplane airliners such as Junkers and Fokkers. Fast and comfortable all-metal airliners, such as the DC-3, were built in the United States during the 1930s. In 1952, the English de Havilland Comet became the first jet airliner, and soon the Boeing 707 was in service all around the world. Airline travel became cheaper and more popular and in 1969 Boeing launched the 747, the first wide-bodied (jumbo-jet) airliner. This is the most successful airliner ever built and by the year 2000, more than 3 billion people will have flown in one. The Boeing 777, however, is waiting in the wings.

BOEING 777
When this sleek, twin-engine airliner rolls off the production line in 1995, it will carry up to 440 people, use less fuel and be much quieter than the 747.

PROPELLED FLIGHT
The Douglas DC-3 (1936) is the most successful propeller-driven airliner. More than 13,000 planes were built and at least 1,000 are still flying.

ARMCHAIR AIRCRAFT
The cabin of a Heracles airliner was designed to resemble the luxury and comfort of the first-class carriage of a railway car.

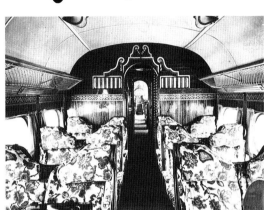

1919 Junkers F/13
This was the first all-metal airliner. It had four seats and could travel at 168 km (104 miles) per hour.

1925 Fokker V11a/3m
This eight-seater was one of the first three-engined airliners. It could travel at 185 km (115 miles) per hour.

1933 Boeing 247D
This was the first streamlined airliner with retractable landing gear. It could carry ten people, and travel at 320 km (198 miles) per hour.

1936 Short C-Class
This float plane flew the route from England to Australia. It had 24 seats and could fly at 320 km (198 miles) per hour.

LOCKHEED ELECTRA
This short-range airliner, which carried 12 passengers, began flying in 1934.

A BUSH BEGINNING
People in the Australian outback town of Winton rush to greet the First World War BE2 biplane, used by the Queensland and Northern Territory Air Service (QANTAS) in 1922.

CAREFUL PACKING
As a safety precaution, airline baggage is X-rayed before being loaded on today's airliners. The X-ray detects any unusual item, such as the pistol in this suitcase.

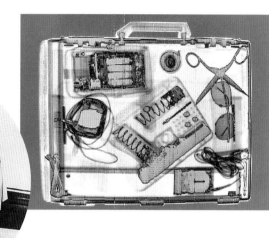

FLIGHT ATTENDANTS
In 1930, United Airlines hired the first airline stewardesses. They were all registered nurses, and all under 25 years of age.

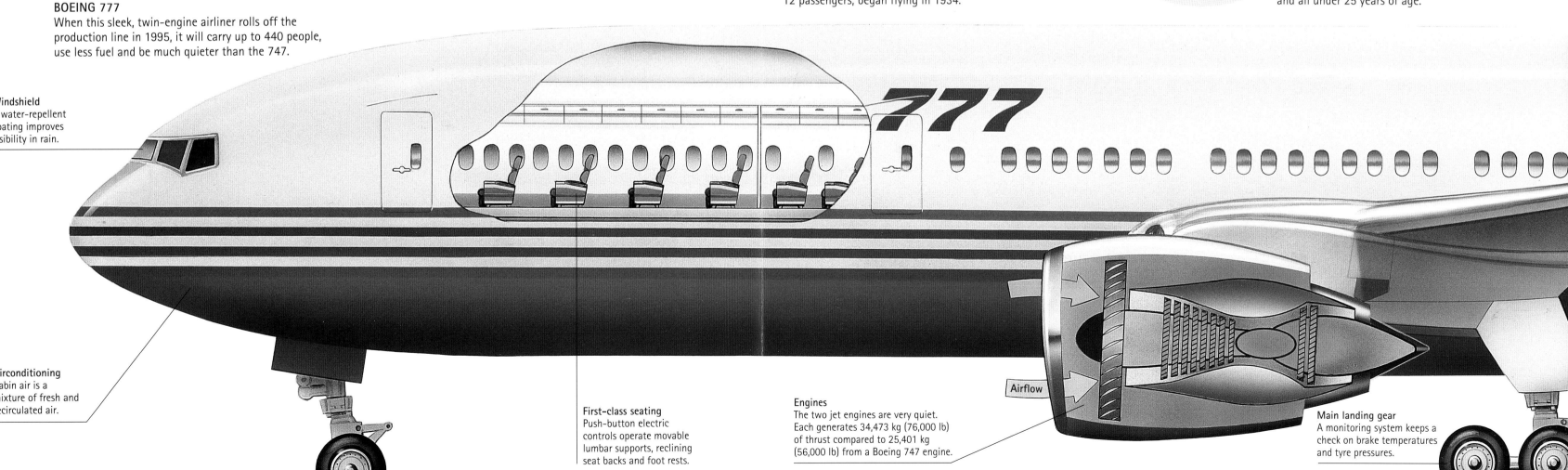

Windshield
A water-repellent coating improves visibility in rain.

Airconditioning
Cabin air is a mixture of fresh and recirculated air.

First-class seating
Push-button electric controls operate movable lumbar supports, reclining seat backs and foot rests.

Engines
The two jet engines are very quiet. Each generates 34,473 kg (76,000 lb) of thrust compared to 25,401 kg (56,000 lb) from a Boeing 747 engine.

Airflow

Main landing gear
A monitoring system keeps a check on brake temperatures and tyre pressures.

Amphibian
This has retractable landing gear and operates from land or water.

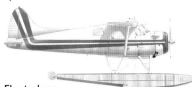

Float plane
This operates only from the water and uses floats.

Flying boat
The large hull of the flying boat is shaped like that of a boat.

GLOBAL TRAVEL

Flying boats were used on the early transoceanic airline services. Pan American Airways pioneered long-range flying boat services in the mid-1930s when its Commodores and S-42s flew to South America and Martin M-130s crossed the Pacific. In 1938, Short S-23s operated the England to Australia service. In 1939, a Boeing 314 made the first transatlantic airline run. Catalinas were used during the Second World War.

Boeing 314

Southampton
Karachi
Hong Kong
Bolama
Perth
Auckland
San Francisco
Honolulu
Miami
Rio de Janeiro
Buenos Aires

Martin M-130

Shorts S.23 Empire

Sikorsky S-42

Consolidated PBY Catalina

Consolidated Commodore

Q: Why were flying boats so popular in the 1930s?

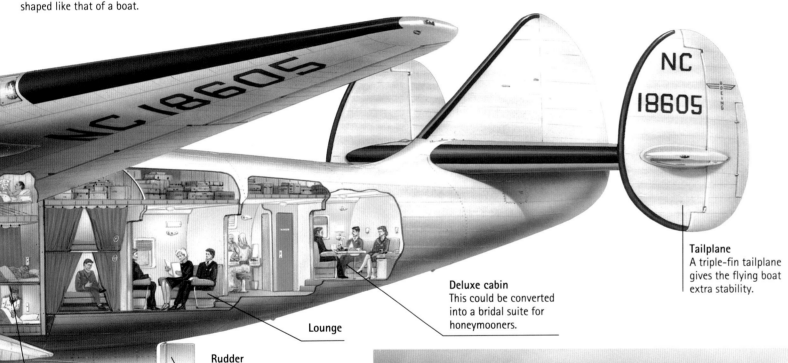

NC 18605

NC 18605

Tailplane
A triple-fin tailplane gives the flying boat extra stability.

Deluxe cabin
This could be converted into a bridal suite for honeymooners.

Lounge

Rudder
This operated like a ship's rudder to steer the plane when it taxied on water.

Day/night cabin
Fold-down bunks in the cabin converted it into sleeping quarters.

A VALUABLE CARGO
The Martin Mars flying boat is used today to fight forest fires. It can skim over water and take 275,000 litres (60,500 gallons) of water on board in 30 seconds.

MIX AND MATCH
In 1925, Juan de la Cierva designed an autogiro, a stepping stone between aeroplanes and helicopters. It could not hover or move sideways, but it could fly very slowly using its windblown rotor.

• A PARADE OF AIRCRAFT •

Helicopters

Helicopters can fly backwards, forwards, sideways, hover in one place and land in the smallest of spaces. They have many advantages over ordinary aeroplanes. The first helicopter and the earliest known powered aircraft was actually a fourteenth-century toy with a four-bladed rotor like a windmill. Leonardo da Vinci, who lived between 1452 and 1519, drew plans for a full-sized helicopter (above left). About four hundred years later, Paul Cornu became the first person to fly in a helicopter. Successful twin-rotor helicopters were produced in Germany during the 1930s, but Igor Sikorsky revolutionised this machine with the design of his single-rotor helicopter after the Second World War. Helicopters have now become part of our lives. They are used as aerial ambulances and cranes; to fight bushfires and to carry out police work; for traffic and shark control, news reporting, cattle herding; and to help rescue people in distress.

SEA RESCUE
The pilot of this Bell JetRanger hovers while the winch operator hauls a rescue victim aboard. Hovering requires very delicate handling of the collective, cyclic and rudder controls. It is a little like trying to pat your head and rub your stomach while balancing on a bowling ball.

Cyclic control
This tilts the whole rotor to move in the desired direction.

Collective control
This changes the angle of the rotor blades. The pilot uses it to climb or descend.

A MOMENT OF FAME
In 1907, French mechanic Paul Cornu hovered 0.3 m (1 ft) off the ground for 20 seconds. But his fragile machine broke into many pieces when he crashed to the ground.

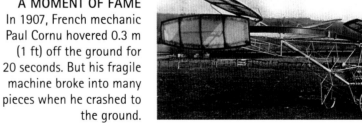

Rudder pedals
These are linked to the small tail rotor, which helps steer the helicopter.

AIRBORNE
Dressed for the occasion, Russian-born Igor Sikorsky sits at the controls of his VS-300. This was the first practical helicopter.

Lockheed Constellation
was the best piston-engine
er. It had 54 seats and could
at 450 km (279 miles) per hour.

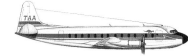

1948 Vickers Viscount
This was the first turboprop-engine
airliner. It had 47 seats and could
travel at 506 km (314 miles) per hour.

1949 de Havilland Comet 1
This was the first jet-engine airliner.
It had 44 seats and travelled at
784 km (486 miles) per hour.

1957 Boeing 707-120
This was the most successful pre-jumbo
jet airliner. It had 143 seats and
travelled at 960 km (595 miles) per hour.

TELL-TAILS
The tailplanes of airliners from
different companies have very
distinct markings, which
makes them easy to recognise.

B-767

B-777

B-747

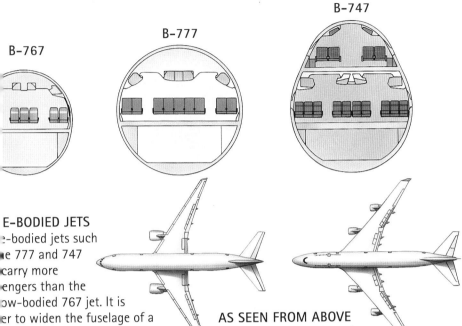

E-BODIED JETS
e-bodied jets such
e 777 and 747
carry more
engers than the
ow-bodied 767 jet. It is
er to widen the fuselage of a
e than lengthen it to create more
e for passengers, as widening
fuselage does not affect the
e's stability.

AS SEEN FROM ABOVE
The 777 is smaller than the
747, but it can carry more
people. It has fewer engines
and is quieter than the 747.

AIR CORRIDORS
A network of invisible aerial highways helps to
control the enormous number of planes in the air.
They are marked on special aviation maps and pilots
use radio, radar and satellite navigation systems to
follow them. Planes in each air corridor must be
60 nautical miles apart. In the same corridor, planes
flying in the same direction and height must be
80 nautical miles apart. If planes are flying at different
heights in the same direction, they must be 1,219 m
(4,000 ft) apart. If they are flying in opposite directions
above 9,144 m (30,000 ft), they must be 610 m
(2,000 ft) apart.

610 m
(2,000 ft)
apart

1,219 m
(4,000 ft)
apart

9,144 m
(30,000) ft

80

60

STORM WARNING
Modern airline pilots
can see storms or
turbulent areas on
their cockpit
radar screen.

TRAFFIC CONTROL
This picture of a radar
screen in air traffic
control shows
aeroplanes flying along
several airways. The tiny
symbols mark each plane's
flight path position.

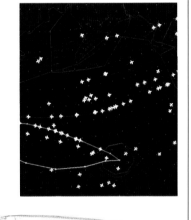

FACTORY SPACE
Boeing 747, 767 and 777 airliners are built in
the largest building in the world—a factory near Seattle in
the United States. It has 14.2 million cubic m
(501$\frac{1}{2}$ million cubic ft) of space.

FLOOR PLAN
A Boeing 777 can carry 302 people if the plane is
divided into the three classes shown. However, it can also be
converted to carry 440 passengers, if they all travel economy class.

Economy class

First class

Business class

Economy class

Fuel tanks
These carry
117,335 litres
(25,814 gallons)
of fuel.

Optional folding wings
The B-777 can use
crowded airports
because 7 m (23 feet)
of each wingtip can
fold up on the ground.

Cargo hold
On long flights, part of
the cargo hold can be
converted to a cabin
rest area with bunks for
off-duty crew.

Main rotor
These are spinning wings that produce the lift to make a helicopter fly.

Tail rotor
This steers the helicopter and prevents it from spinning in the opposite direction to the main rotor.

Rescue winch
This electrically powered winch lifts people and supplies up and down.

Q: Why are helicopters used for many rescue missions?

THE WORKINGS OF A HELICOPTER

A helicopter has a set of spinning wings called a rotor. This provides the lift force and controls the helicopter's direction. The rotor is connected to collective pitch and cyclic pitch levers, which the pilot uses to control the helicopter. The small tail rotor holds the helicopter body in a straight line.

Ascending
The pilot raises the collective pitch lever. This steepens the rotor-blade angle until the lift force is more than the helicopter's weight.

Descending
The pilot lowers the collective pitch lever. This decreases the rotor-blade angle until the lift force is less than the helicopter's weight.

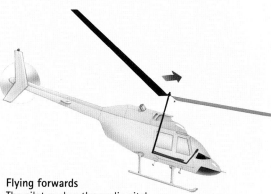

Flying forwards
The pilot pushes the cyclic pitch control forward. This causes the rotor to tilt down at the front, which divides the lift force and provides forward thrust.

Flying sideways
The pilot moves the cyclic pitch control sideways. The rotor tilts sideways, dividing the lift force again and providing a sideways force.

• A PARADE OF AIRCRAFT •

Planes at Work

Pilots were inventive in the ways they used their wonderful new flying machines. In 1911, Frenchman Henri Pequet began an airmail service in India. Two weeks later, similar services were started in France, Italy and the United States. During the First World War, a French company built a huge biplane, which contained a portable operating theatre. It landed on the battlefields carrying surgeons and nurses, who carried out emergency operations amid the chaos of war. The Huff Daland Dusters began dusting crops from aeroplanes in country areas of the United States in 1924. When goldmines were built in New Guinea, all the supplies and materials were delivered by adventurous bush pilots. They landed on dangerous airstrips, carved from the jungle, in Junkers monoplanes. As the world's aeroplane industry grew, so too did the jobs aeroplanes performed. They are now used to fight fires; herd cattle; guard coasts and look for sharks; drop supplies to the victims of floods, storms and famines; and carry cargo.

A CLEAR VIEW
The slow-flying Edgely EA 7 Optica has a glass cockpit. This makes it ideal as an aerial spotter.

AIR WATCH
The coastlines in America are patrolled by specially equip observation planes, such as this high-speed Falcon jet.

ON THE LAND
Helicopters are efficient and effective alternatives to traditional ways of rounding up horses and cattle.

AERIAL PACKHORSE
The giant Hercules is the best known flying packhorse. Its enormous rear door makes it easy to load and unload cargo. It can also be opened in flight if supplies need to be dropped by parachute. This Hercules is delivering food to a community in Africa.

48

THE FLYING DOCTORS

The Royal Flying Doctor Service cares for the families who live in Australia's desolate outback. The first flying doctor flew in a slow de Havilland biplane, with an open cockpit. Today, the service uses twin-engine Beech Kingair passenger planes, which cruise at 442 km (274 miles) per hour. The doctors and nurses are on stand-by day and night for emergency calls. Their territory covers 5 million sq km (2 million sq miles), but they can reach any part of it within two hours. Every bush town and isolated homestead has a radio transmitter to call the flying doctor bases. When the service first began in 1928, these radios were run by the pedal-powered generators shown here.

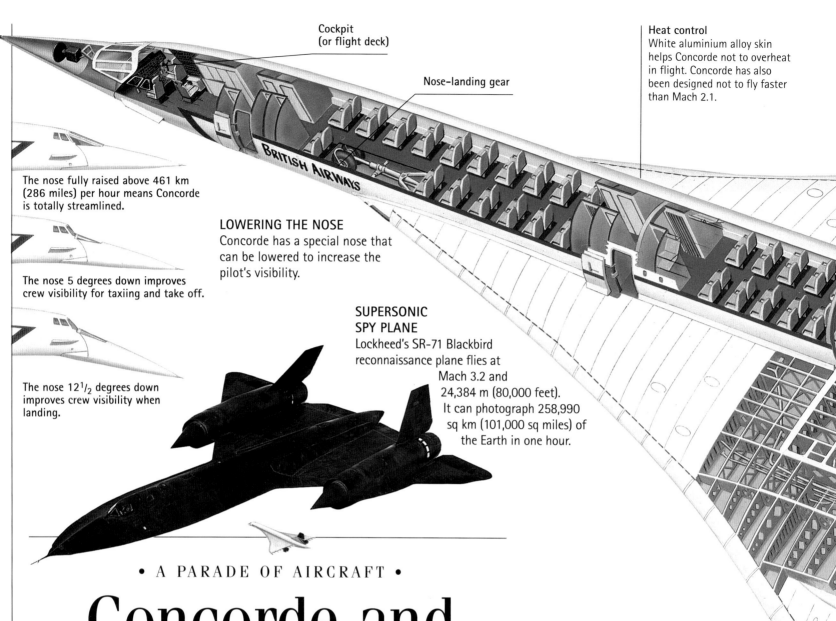

Cockpit
(or flight deck)

Nose-landing gear

Heat control
White aluminium alloy skin
helps Concorde not to overheat
in flight. Concorde has also
been designed not to fly faster
than Mach 2.1.

BRITISH AIRWAYS

The nose fully raised above 461 km
(286 miles) per hour means Concorde
is totally streamlined.

The nose 5 degrees down improves
crew visibility for taxiing and take off.

The nose 12$^{1}/_{2}$ degrees down
improves crew visibility when
landing.

LOWERING THE NOSE
Concorde has a special nose that
can be lowered to increase the
pilot's visibility.

**SUPERSONIC
SPY PLANE**
Lockheed's SR-71 Blackbird
reconnaissance plane flies at
Mach 3.2 and
24,384 m (80,000 feet).
It can photograph 258,990
sq km (101,000 sq miles) of
the Earth in one hour.

• A PARADE OF AIRCRAFT •

Concorde and Supersonic Flight

In the 1960s, Britain and France joined forces to develop a passenger plane that could fly at the speed of sound—a supersonic airliner. The Americans also began to design such a plane, but they abandoned it when costs skyrocketed and concentrated instead on building large subsonic jumbo jets. In 1969, Concorde, the world's first commercial supersonic plane, made its debut flight. The 14-plane Concorde fleet started service with British Airways and Air France in 1976. By then, the Soviet Union had built a supersonic airliner called the Tu-114. It crashed tragically at an airshow and never flew passenger services. Concorde has not been a great commerical success. It is expensive to operate, seats only 100 passengers, and is banned from many cities because of its sonic boom. It is, however, a technological triumph. Cruising at twice the speed of sound, Concorde can fly from New York to London in three-and-a-half hours.

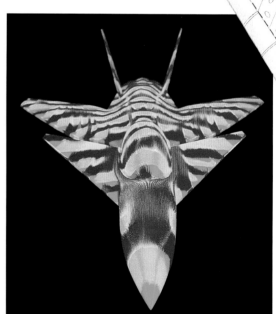

WIND TUNNELS
Aeroplanes are tested in wind tunnels, which imitate the airflow they will experience in flight. This model is covered with fluorescent paint, which will highlight the airflow and any problem areas.

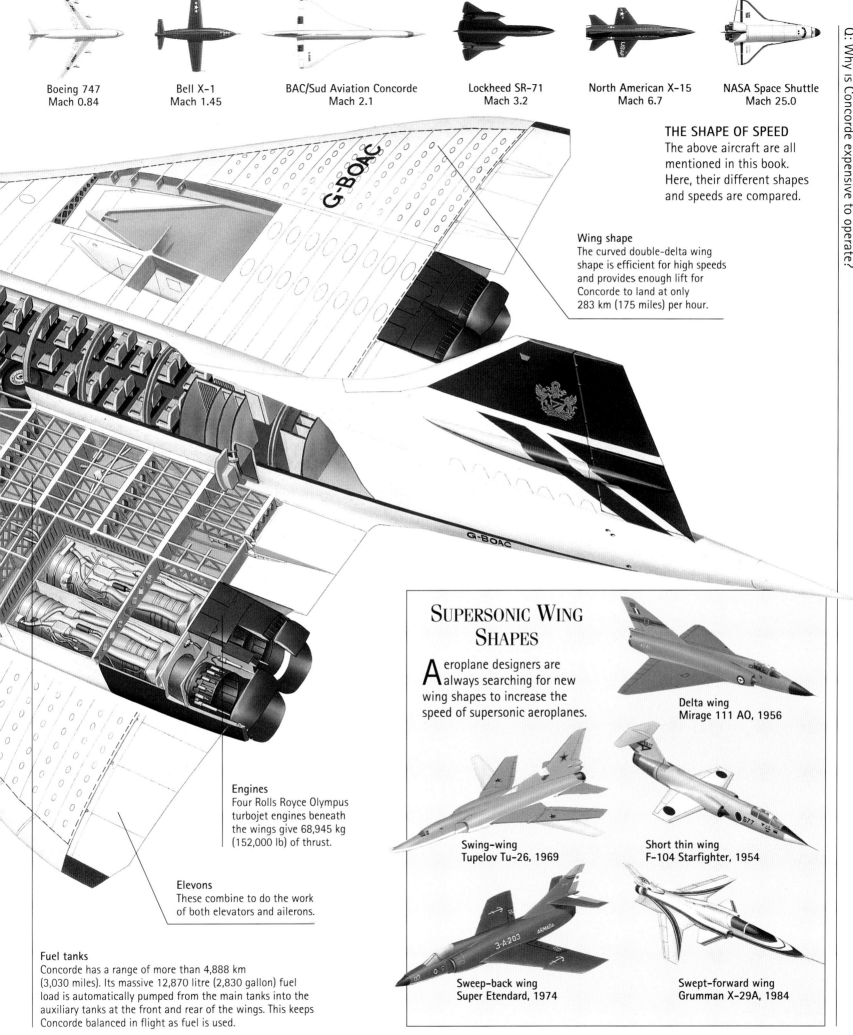

Boeing 747
Mach 0.84

Bell X-1
Mach 1.45

BAC/Sud Aviation Concorde
Mach 2.1

Lockheed SR-71
Mach 3.2

North American X-15
Mach 6.7

NASA Space Shuttle
Mach 25.0

THE SHAPE OF SPEED

The above aircraft are all mentioned in this book. Here, their different shapes and speeds are compared.

Wing shape

The curved double-delta wing shape is efficient for high speeds and provides enough lift for Concorde to land at only 283 km (175 miles) per hour.

Engines

Four Rolls Royce Olympus turbojet engines beneath the wings give 68,945 kg (152,000 lb) of thrust.

Elevons

These combine to do the work of both elevators and ailerons.

Fuel tanks

Concorde has a range of more than 4,888 km (3,030 miles). Its massive 12,870 litre (2,830 gallon) fuel load is automatically pumped from the main tanks into the auxiliary tanks at the front and rear of the wings. This keeps Concorde balanced in flight as fuel is used.

SUPERSONIC WING SHAPES

Aeroplane designers are always searching for new wing shapes to increase the speed of supersonic aeroplanes.

Delta wing
Mirage 111 AO, 1956

Swing-wing
Tupelov Tu-26, 1969

Short thin wing
F-104 Starfighter, 1954

Sweep-back wing
Super Etendard, 1974

Swept-forward wing
Grumman X-29A, 1984

51

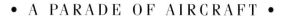

Military Aircraft

Wars have accelerated the development of aircraft. At the beginning of the First World War, most planes could not fly further than 161 km (100 miles) and had a maximum speed of around 100 km (62 miles) per hour. The first military planes were used only for observing enemy activity from the air, but they were soon adapted for fighting. By the end of the war, bombers could travel almost 3,220 km (2,000 miles) and reach speeds of 241 km (150 miles) per hour. The most famous war planes of the Second World War were the piston-engine Spitfire, Mustang and Messerschmitt 109 fighters, the Flying Fortress and Lancaster bombers. Rocket-powered planes and jet fighters were also introduced, and the first all-jet air battle took place during the 1950–53 Korean War. Military planes today are controlled by onboard computers and can fly at supersonic speeds.

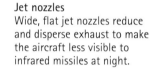

Jet nozzles
Wide, flat jet nozzles reduce and disperse exhaust to make the aircraft less visible to infrared missiles at night.

AIR-TO-AIR MISSILES
Modern fighter pilots do not even need to see their enemy. They can destroy other aircraft with deadly missiles guided by electronic or infrared devices.

UNDETECTABLE
Lockheed's F-117A Stealth Fighter is designed to be invisible on enemy radar screens. Most aeroplanes are rounded, but the surfaces of this plane are faceted (like a diamond) and highly polished to deflect and disperse radar signals.

A TIMELY EXIT
A pilot escapes in a rocket-powered ejection seat as his fighter explodes. Moments later, a parachute will open and bring him safely to the ground.

1915 German Fokker E.1 Eindecker
This could fly at 128 km (79 miles) per hour and was the first fighter equipped with a proper forward-firing machine gun.

1917 French Spad X11
This great biplane fighter was flown by French, American and British airmen. It could fly at 208 km (129 miles) per hour.

1917 English Handley Page 0/400
This giant bomber could carry a 906-kg (2,002-lb) load of bombs and travel at 128 km (79 miles) per hour.

1938 English Supermarine Spitfire
More than 20,000 Supermarine Spitfires were built during the Second World War. This model could fly at 576 km (357 miles) per hour.

JUMP JETS

This McDonnell Douglas AV-8B version of the British Harrier jump jet is flown by the United States Marine Corps. It is called a V/STOL (Vertical/Short Take Off and Landing) aeroplane because it can hover, land and take off like a helicopter. Its jet exhausts shoot out horizontally to the rear like an ordinary fighter plane when it is flying normally. The jet nozzles direct the exhaust vertically downwards for landing and taking off. The Harrier takes a short run to help it "jump" into the air when it has a heavy load.

VIEWING ON SCREEN

When fighter pilots are in combat, they need to be able to look around and react quickly. Important instrument information is displayed on the visor of this special helmet, which means the pilot does not have to look down at the instrument panel.

V-tail
This V-tail replaces the usual vertical and horizontal tailplanes. It is slanted back to deflect or inhibit enemy radar and infrared sensors.

Cockpit
Serrated edges around the cockpit deflect enemy radar.

Infrared sensor
A grill covers the F-117A's own infrared sensors and deflects radar.

Smart bombs
Two laser-guided smart bombs are carried internally in the fuselage.

Engine intake
Engine air inlets have grids to disperse enemy radar.

Faceted pilot tubes
These provide airspeed and altitude readings for the pilot.

1943 English Gloster Meteor
This was powered by two engines and was the first British jet fighter. It could fly at 969 km (600 miles) per hour.

1952 United States Boeing B-52 Stratofortress
This giant bomber was powered by eight jets and flew a record 20,034 km (12,421 miles). It could fly at 960 km (595 miles) per hour.

1974 German, English and Italian Panavia Tornado
This strike aircraft has variable sweep wings. It can travel at 2,333 km (1,446 miles) per hour.

1978 United States McDonnell Douglas F/A 18C Hornet
This is also used by Australia, Canada, Spain and Kuwait. It can fly at 2,124 km (1,317 miles) per hour.

Aircraft Carriers

COUNTING DOWN
The plane is in launch position on the carrier. The catapult crew, wearing green jackets, are in place. The catapult officer (the "shooter"), wearing a yellow jacket, gives the signal to launch the plane.

A coal barge was the first, and perhaps most unlikely, aircraft carrier. It towed observation balloons during the American Civil War. In 1910, American stunt pilot Eugene Ely flew his Curtiss biplane from a platform on the cruiser USS *Birmingham*. The first true carrier, however, was built by the British during the First World War. Its narrow landing deck was very dangerous and returning pilots were forbidden to land. They had to ditch their planes in the sea. Aircraft carriers did improve, and by the Second World War they had replaced battleships as the most important naval ships. The bombers from a Japanese carrier force made a devastating attack on Pearl Harbour in 1941, and the major sea battles in the Pacific were fought by squadrons of carrier-based planes. Today, huge nuclear-powered carriers are the most powerful ships in the world.

THE LANDING PATTERN
Carrier pilots fly 8-km (5-mile) wide circles at different heights while "hawking" (watching) the carrier, waiting to land. When the last aircraft are ready to launch, the pilots take turns to join the approach pattern. They time their descent to land the moment the deck is clear.

LAUNCHING
A holdback device on the catapult's shuttle (launcher) stops a plane rolling forward, even when it is under full power, until the catapult is fired.

Jet-blast deflector
Retractable steel walls deflect the jet exhaust away from the deck.

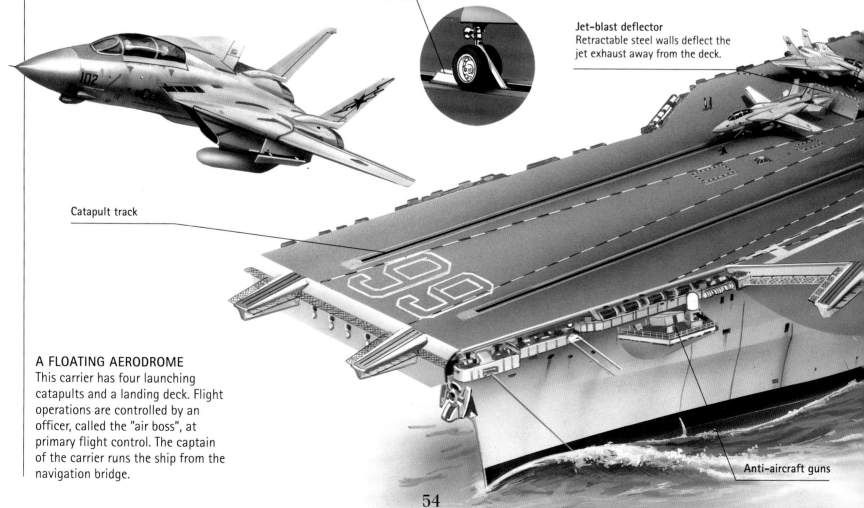

Catapult track

A FLOATING AERODROME
This carrier has four launching catapults and a landing deck. Flight operations are controlled by an officer, called the "air boss", at primary flight control. The captain of the carrier runs the ship from the navigation bridge.

Anti-aircraft guns

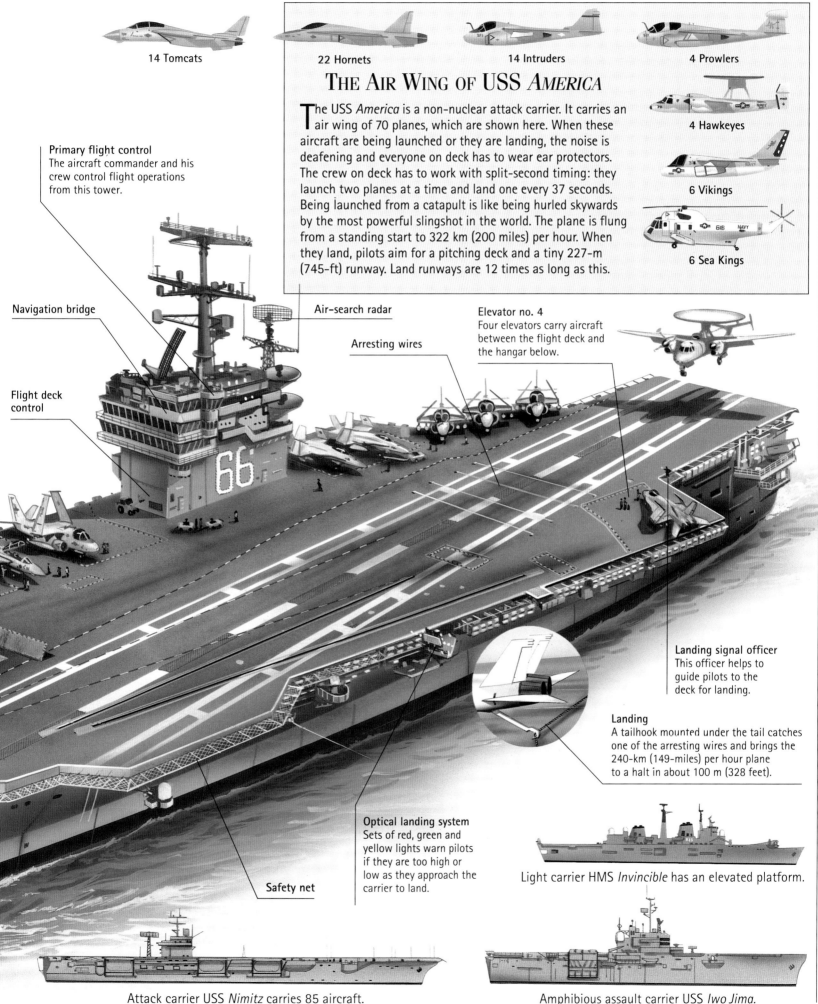

14 Tomcats

22 Hornets

14 Intruders

4 Prowlers

4 Hawkeyes

6 Vikings

6 Sea Kings

THE AIR WING OF USS AMERICA

The USS *America* is a non-nuclear attack carrier. It carries an air wing of 70 planes, which are shown here. When these aircraft are being launched or they are landing, the noise is deafening and everyone on deck has to wear ear protectors. The crew on deck has to work with split-second timing: they launch two planes at a time and land one every 37 seconds. Being launched from a catapult is like being hurled skywards by the most powerful slingshot in the world. The plane is flung from a standing start to 322 km (200 miles) per hour. When they land, pilots aim for a pitching deck and a tiny 227-m (745-ft) runway. Land runways are 12 times as long as this.

Primary flight control
The aircraft commander and his crew control flight operations from this tower.

Navigation bridge

Flight deck control

Air-search radar

Arresting wires

Elevator no. 4
Four elevators carry aircraft between the flight deck and the hangar below.

Landing signal officer
This officer helps to guide pilots to the deck for landing.

Landing
A tailhook mounted under the tail catches one of the arresting wires and brings the 240-km (149-miles) per hour plane to a halt in about 100 m (328 feet).

Safety net

Optical landing system
Sets of red, green and yellow lights warn pilots if they are too high or low as they approach the carrier to land.

Light carrier HMS *Invincible* has an elevated platform.

Attack carrier USS *Nimitz* carries 85 aircraft.

Amphibious assault carrier USS *Iwo Jima*.

Goddard 1926 (USA)
First successful liquid-propellant rocket travelled 56 m (184 feet).

V-2 1942 (Germany)
First successful military rocket and reached an altitude of 85 km (53 miles).

Sputnik I 1957 (Russia)
First satellite to go into orbit. It carried a radio transmitter.

Hubble telescope 1990 (USA)
Space telescope was launched into orbit.

Gagarin 1961 (Russia)
First person in space. His spaceship was called *Vostok 1*.

Columbia 1981 (USA)
The world's first reusable space shuttle was launched into space.

Viking 1976 (USA)
Viking I and *II* set down on Mars and discovered no signs of life.

Skylab 1973 (USA)
Allowed people to live in space for several weeks.

Armstrong 1969 (USA)
Neil Armstrong was the first person to set foot on the moon.

• A PARADE OF AIRCRAFT •

Space

S pace is an unknown but challenging territory. Since the thirteenth century, when the Chinese first used rocket power, people have been slowly acquiring the knowledge and technology to make travel in space possible. In 1903, Russian Konstantin Tsiolkovsky proposed using liquid-fuel rockets for space travel. American Robert Goddard successfully launched the first liquid-fuelled rocket in 1926. Forty-three years later, *Apollo 11* was launched using the biggest rocket ever built. It carried astronauts Neil Armstrong, Edwin Aldrin and Michael Collins and their lunar lander *Eagle* to the moon. Millions of people all over the world listened to Armstrong's voice, crackling with static, announce that this was a "giant leap for mankind". In 1981, the first reusable space shuttle *Columbia* made 37 orbits of the world. This machine lifts off like a rocket, circles the Earth like a satellite, then uses its wings to glide back to Earth.

WORKING IN SPACE
During a 1994 shuttle mission, astronaut Kathryn Thornton made repairs to the Hubble space telescope.

WEATHER REPORT
This cloudless picture of Europe and North Africa is made up of several photographs. They were taken by cameras aboard weather satellites orbiting the Earth in space.

FLIGHT OF THE SHUTTLE

Three rocket engines and two booster rockets, with power equal to 140 jumbo jets, lift the shuttle off its launch pad and place it into orbit at 28,175 km (17,468 miles) per hour.

Two minutes after launch and 45 km (28 miles) up into the sky, the rocket boosters are released and parachute back to Earth.

At 112 km (69 miles) the main 700-tonne (686-ton) fuel tank falls away and burns up. It re-enters the Earth's atmosphere as the shuttle heads into orbit.

RE-ENTRY
Coming out of orbit, the shuttle slows down to re-enter the Earth's atmosphere. It glides to a landing and touches down at 346 km (215 miles) per hour.

DID YOU KNOW?
Each booster rocket contains 907,184 kg (2 million lb) of aluminium powder that steadily burns over two minutes. The tremendous heat and pressure generated is blasted from the rocket nozzle and causes the shuttle to lift.

USA

United States

NASA
Atlantis

57

Flights of Tomorrow

Can you imagine the aeroplanes of the future? Will passenger jumbo jets be equipped with shops, restaurants, cabins and space for 1,000 passengers? How fast will the aeroplanes of tomorrow be able to travel? Supersonic planes such as Concorde are the fastest passenger planes today. They travel at Mach 2.2, and to exceed this, airliners would need to fly at about 18,288 m (60,000 feet). But at this high altitude, jet engines can harm the ozone layer. Supersonic planes are also very costly to build and this makes it expensive to travel on them. Special-purpose aeroplanes such as the Bell/Boeing Tiltrotor, which is part-helicopter and part-aeroplane, will definitely be part of aviation's future. This aircraft can fly between cities, land in tiny downtown airports and on the roofs of buildings. But what will be the ultimate flight of tomorrow? Perhaps flying to space in a space-shuttle airliner.

PICTURE THIS!
Boeing has imagined a supersonic airliner of the 21st century. It could carry about 300 people nonstop for 9,600 km (6,000 miles) at the same speed as Concorde today.

FLYING INTO THE FUTURE
A tiltrotor airliner takes off from a landing pad, or vertiport, on a Hong Kong rooftop. These 200-passenger planes of the future will hover like helicopters, whisk between cities at 550 km (341 miles) per hour, and help to reduce congestion at the crowded airports of tomorrow.

UPSTAIRS, DOWNSTAIRS
This two-storey jumbo of the future will fly at about the same speed as a Boeing 747, but it will be able to carry more than 500 passengers.

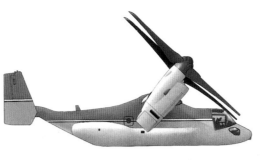

THE FLIGHT STAGES OF A TILTROTOR
It uses its rotors to take off (or land) vertically, like a helicopter.

It tilts its rotors and starts to move forwards.

The tilt rotors operate as normal propellers and it flies like an aeroplane.

TOGETHER TO MARS

The United States and Russia are working on an exciting program called "Mars Together". In the late 1990s, American and Russian rockets will launch a series of robot spacecraft, which will orbit, land and explore the surface of the Red Planet. In another program called "Fire and Ice", the two nations will explore the sun and the planet Pluto.

Completing the Picture

It is difficult to get a really good view of an aeroplane when it is on the ground or flying noisily overhead. This page, however, shows three-way views of 12 of the aeroplanes that have appeared as main images in this book. A three-way view is a standard aviation drawing that allows you to inspect and identify the plane's vital statistics: its shape; the number, type and position of the engines; and its wingspan.

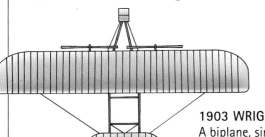

1903 WRIGHT *FLYER*
A biplane, single-piston engine.
Max speed: approx 48 km (30 miles) per hour.
Wingspan: 12.3 m (40 feet).

GRAF ZEPPELIN
An airship, five piston engines.
Max speed: 128 km (79 miles) per hour.
Length: 236 m (774 feet).

SUPERMARINE S.5
A monoplane float plane, single-piston engine.
Max speed: 451 km (280 miles) per hour.
Wingspan: 8.4 m (27$\frac{1}{2}$ feet).

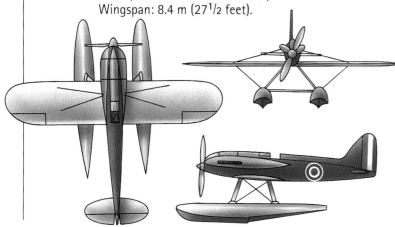

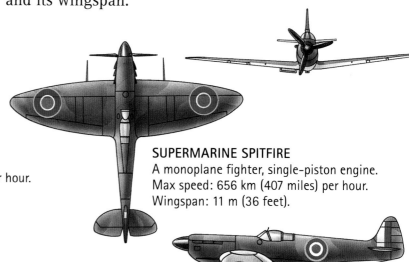

SUPERMARINE SPITFIRE
A monoplane fighter, single-piston engine.
Max speed: 656 km (407 miles) per hour.
Wingspan: 11 m (36 feet).

BOEING 314 CLIPPER
A monoplane flying boat, four piston engines.
Max speed: 309 km (192 miles) per hour.
Wingspan: 43 m (141 feet).

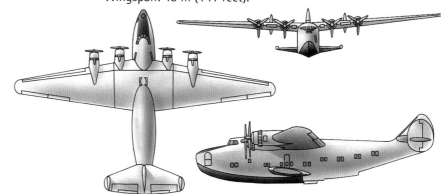

BELL X-1
An experimental monoplane, single-rocket motor.
Max speed: Mach 1.45, 1,531 km (949 miles) per hour.
Wingspan: 8.5 m (28 feet).

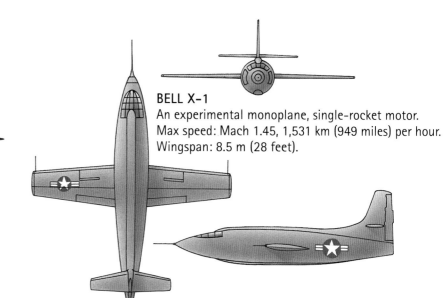

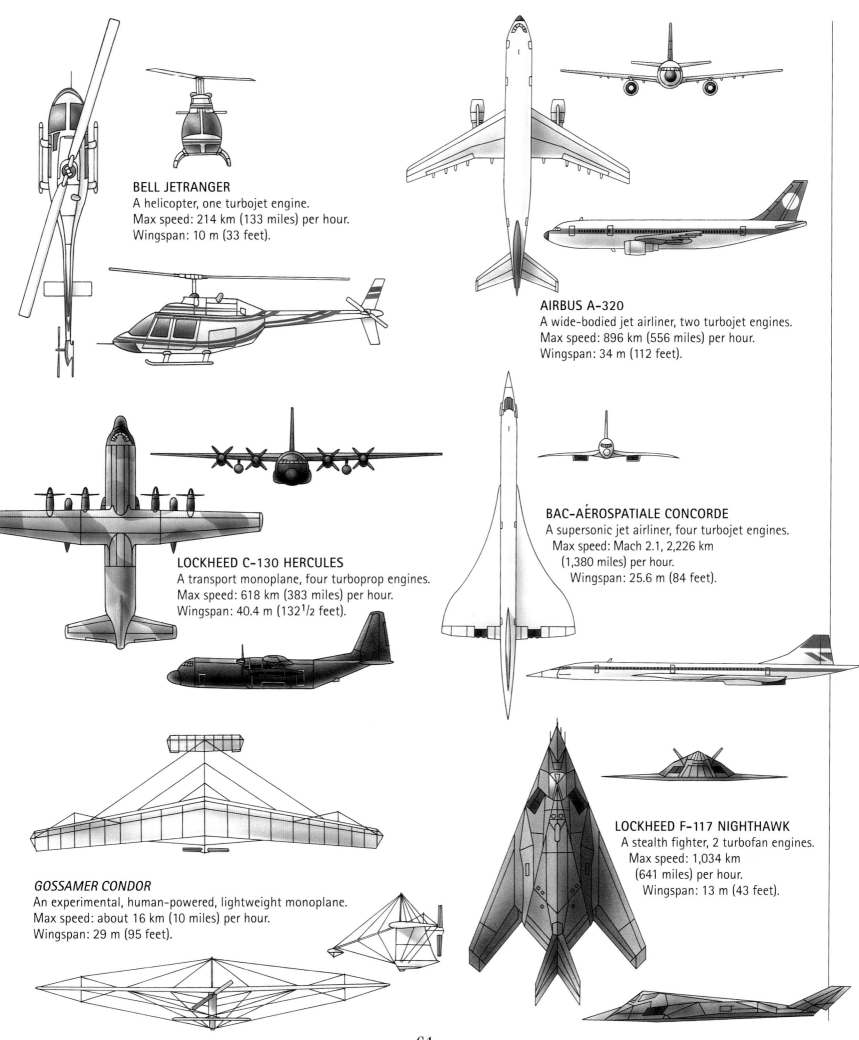

BELL JETRANGER
A helicopter, one turbojet engine.
Max speed: 214 km (133 miles) per hour.
Wingspan: 10 m (33 feet).

AIRBUS A-320
A wide-bodied jet airliner, two turbojet engines.
Max speed: 896 km (556 miles) per hour.
Wingspan: 34 m (112 feet).

LOCKHEED C-130 HERCULES
A transport monoplane, four turboprop engines.
Max speed: 618 km (383 miles) per hour.
Wingspan: 40.4 m (132$\frac{1}{2}$ feet).

BAC-AÉROSPATIALE CONCORDE
A supersonic jet airliner, four turbojet engines.
Max speed: Mach 2.1, 2,226 km
(1,380 miles) per hour.
Wingspan: 25.6 m (84 feet).

GOSSAMER CONDOR
An experimental, human-powered, lightweight monoplane.
Max speed: about 16 km (10 miles) per hour.
Wingspan: 29 m (95 feet).

LOCKHEED F-117 NIGHTHAWK
A stealth fighter, 2 turbofan engines.
Max speed: 1,034 km
(641 miles) per hour.
Wingspan: 13 m (43 feet).

Glossary

Mythical Garuda bird

Aerial Steam Carriage

Butterfly

Wilbur and Orville Wright

Space shuttle

aerodynamics The science that deals with air and how aircraft fly.

aerofoil A structure such as a wing, a tailplane or a propeller blade that develops lift when moving quickly through the air.

aeroplane A powered, heavier-than-air aircraft.

ailerons Movable controls fixed to the wings that are used to make an aeroplane bank.

airflow The flow of air past a moving aircraft.

airship A lighter-than-air aircraft that is driven by an engine and able to be steered.

airstream A current of moving air.

altitude An aviation term for height.

angle of attack The angle at which the wing meets the airstream.

area rule A special way of designing the shape of an aeroplane to reduce drag when it flies at supersonic speeds.

autogiro An aeroplane that gets lift from an unpowered rotor.

autopilot A system that keeps an aeroplane flying automatically at an altitude (height) and heading (direction) chosen by the pilot.

balloon An unsteerable aircraft that is lighter-than-air.

balloon basket This holds the pilot, passengers and flight instruments.

banking When the pilot lowers one wing and raises the other during a turn.

biplane A fixed-wing aeroplane with two sets of wings.

buffeting The shaking and bumping of an aeroplane as it nears the speed of sound (Mach 1.0) and is affected by shock waves.

catapult A powerful, steam-powered device that launches aeroplanes from aircraft carriers.

cockpit The compartment where the pilot or crew sit to control the aircraft.

collective pitch The control that makes a helicopter climb and descend.

cyclic pitch The control that makes a helicopter move in a horizontal direction.

dihedral The angle at which wings or tailplanes are attached to the fuselage. It helps to keep the aeroplane stable.

drag The resistance caused by the shape of an aircraft to its movement through the air.

ejection seat A rocket-powered seat that fires (or ejects) the pilot out of an aeroplane. The pilot then parachutes to safety.

elevator A movable control fixed to the tailplane that makes an aeroplane climb or descend.

fin The fixed, vertical part of the tail unit that helps keep an aeroplane flying straight ahead (also called the vertical stabiliser).

float plane A seaplane that is supported on the water by floats.

flying boat A seaplane that is supported on the water by its fuselage.

flying circuses Groups of pilots who banded together in the early years of flying to perform aerial tricks and stunts for the public.

fuselage The body of an aircraft.

gas burners Burners that are fed by propane gas to provide the heat that lifts a hot-air balloon.

glider An unpowered, heavier-than-air aircraft.

gondola The passenger and crew cabin of an airship.

helicopter An aircraft that gets its lift from a powered rotor.

infrared missiles Rocket-powered missiles that are guided to their target by an infrared homing system. They detect objects in a way that is similar to the automatic focusing system used on many automatic cameras.

jetstream Winds exceeding 160 km (99 miles) per hour that blow at very high altitudes.

joyflights When people pay to fly in small aeroplanes to experience the excitement of flying.

kite A tethered glider that is lifted by the wind. A kite was the first heavier-than-air aircraft.

landing gear The name for the wheels that support an aeroplane on the ground. It is also called the "undercarriage".

lift The upward force created when the airstream passes around an aerofoil (such as a wing, a tailplane or a propeller blade).

Mach number The speed of an aeroplane compared with the speed of sound. Mach 1.0 is the speed of sound. A plane that flies at Mach 0.75 is flying at 75 per cent of the speed of sound.

monoplane A fixed-wing aeroplane with one set of wings.

orbit To circle the earth, another planet or a star in space.

pitching The aerodynamic term used to describe an aeroplane's nose moving up and down.

primary feathers A bird's outermost wing feathers that provide the thrust for flight.

propeller A set of blades driven by an engine that pull or push an aeroplane through the air. It is sometimes called an airscrew.

pylon racing Air racing close to the ground around a course marked by painted pylons.

radar A method of using radio beams for navigation, or to show up other objects in the air.

reconnaissance plane An aircraft that is designed to take pictures, and sometimes to spy over enemy territory.

rolling The aerodynamic term used to describe an aeroplane banking—when one wing lifts and the other drops down.

rotors Two or more long narrow wings (called blades) that provide lift for a helicopter or an autogiro.

rudder A movable control fixed to the fin that helps control direction.

sailplane A high performance glider designed specially to soar on thermals.

sonic boom A sound like a thunderclap that is sometimes heard on the ground. It is caused by the shock waves from a supersonic aircraft.

sound barrier An invisible, aerodynamic barrier that was once thought to prevent aeroplanes travelling faster than the speed of sound.

space shuttle A reusable aircraft that is used to travel into space.

speed of sound At high altitudes, this is 1,065 km (662 miles) per hour; at sea level the speed of sound is 1,223 km (760 miles) per hour.

stability A plane needs to be stable when it flies. Its wings, fuselage and tailplanes make it easy, safe and smooth to fly.

stalling This happens when a plane flies too slowly. Its wings are unable to produce enough lift and it loses height.

streamlining This gives an aircraft a smooth shape to reduce its air resistance, or drag.

subsonic Flying at less than the speed of sound.

supersonic Flying faster than the speed of sound.

tailplane The fixed, horizontal part of the tail unit that helps to keep an aeroplane stable (also called the horizontal stabiliser).

thermal A column of rising air used by gliders and birds to gain height.

throttle Like the accelerator of a car, this controls the speed of an aeroplane's engine.

thrust The force developed by a propeller or jet engine that drives an aeroplane through the air.

transonic Flying through the sound barrier.

V/STOL Vertical and/or short take off and landing.

wing flap A hinged section of the wing that is lowered when landing and taking off to increase lift at low speed.

wing slat A small aerofoil that forms a gap at the front of the wing to increase lift at low speed.

yawing The aerodynamic term that describes an aeroplane's nose swinging from side to side.

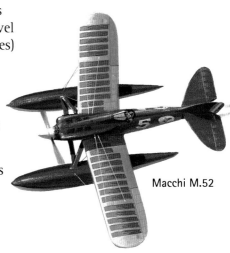

Grob 115

Macchi M.52

DC.3 Dakota

Flying lizard

Float plane

63

Index

Picture Credits

(t=top, b=bottom, l=left, r=right, c=centre, F=front, C=cover, B=back, Bg=background)
Air Portraits, 48tr AKG. Berlin, 6cl, 18bl. **Auckland Museum**, 16br. **Auscape**, 8tr (Hans & Judy Beste), 10bl, 11tr, 63br (J. P. Ferrero). **Austral International**, 20tl, 21t, 42c, 62tl (L'Illustration/Sygma), 24tr (Rex Feature Ltd), 52bl (R. Richards/Liaison/Gamma), 48bl (P. Schofield /Shooting Star. **Australian Geographic**, 19bl (Courtesy P. Smith). **Australian Picture Library**, 56t, 42b (ACME/Bettmann),22br, 62bl (Bettmann), 17tr (B. Desestres /Agence Vandystadt), 33bl (G. Hall), 29br, 30bl (UPI/Bettmann). **Boeing**, 35tl, 58tr, 58bl. **Check Six**, 31br, 33br (M. Fizer), 34tr, 50c, 54tr (G. Hall), 43tr (R. Neville), 48cr (J. Towers). **CSIRO**, Division of Plant Industry, 12br. **Budd Davisson**, 28tl. **Chris Elfes**, 16/17c. **FAA Oceanic Programme**, 46cr. **Enrico Ferorelli**, 15bl. **Werner Forman Archive**, 14tl, 62tl (Denpasar Museum). **The Granger Collection**, 14bl, 15tr, 15br, 25cr, 26tl. **Terry Gwynn-Jones**, 7tl, 23tl, 25br, 26tr, 40tr, 44tl, 44c, 49tl (Royal Flying Doctor Service). **The Image Bank**, 36c (T. Bieber), 36tr (S. Proehl). **Image Select**, 21cr

(Ann Ronan Picture Library). **Imax Corporation**, 13br. **International Photo Library**, 52l. **Lockheed**, 50br. **NASA**, 56tl, 56cl, 56br, 59cr. **NHPA**, 8l (G. I. Bernard), 12tl, 13tr, 62cl (S. Dalton). **North Wind Picture Archives**, 15cr. **Oxford Scientific Films**, 10tl (S. Osolinski). **The Photo Library, Sydney**, 8 cl (J. Burgess / SPL) 56tr (J. Fitzgerald), 57tl (GEOSPACE / SPL), 63cr (D. N. Green), 27cr, 56tr (Hulton-Deutsch), 35tr (J. King-Holmes / SPL), 46tl (P. Poulides / TSI), 56tr, 56c, 56tl, 56/57c (SPL / NASA). **Quadrant**, 44cr, 46cl, 46br, 28bl, 29tr, 42t, 44cl (Flight). **Robert Harding Picture Library**, 56cr. **Royal Aeronautical Society**, 19c, 43cr. **Phil Schofield**, 41br. **Science & Society Picture Library**, 17bl, 21br, 31tr, 42tl (The Science Museum). **SEXTANT Avionique**, 53cr. **Smithsonian Institution**, 23r (Photo no.A42363C), 23br (Photo no.A4943), 25cl (Photo no.75-12199), 25tr (Photo no.89–923), 26c (Photo no.79-763), 29cr (Photo no.93-5512), 30c (Photo no.77-11329), 40bl (Photo no.72-7669). **Topham Picture Source**, 27tr. **TRH Pictures**, 38tr (US Navy) 56tl (NASA). **Visions**, 27tl (M. Greenberg).

Illustration Credits

Christer Ericksson, 18–19c, 48–49. Alan Ewart, FCbl, 34–35. Greg Gillespie, 14–15. Mike Gorman, 11r. Terry Hadler, 2–3b, 5br, 54–55. Langdon G. Halls, FCtr, BCbl, 7br, 23b, 23tr, 30–31, 32–33, 50–51, 52–53b, 53tr, 63tr, David Kirshner, FCtl, 4tl, 4–5t and b, 6–7c, 6tl, 7cr, 8–9, 10–11, 11b, 13c Mike Lamble, 39r, 27br, 59t Alex Lavroff, 5t, 52–53 Kent Leech, 38–39, 39t Ulrich Lehmann, 43–46 Oliver Rennert, 36–37 John Richards, 5r, 20–21, 24–25, 28–29, 63tr, Trevor Ruth, 1, 4bl, 22–23, 12–13, 58–59 Steve Seymour, 2tl, 42–43, 40–41 Ray Sim, 26–27b Steve Trevaskis, icons, 6br, 7bl, 16–17, 19br, Ross Watton/Garden Studio, 57tr, 57cr, 62bl Rod Westblade, 35c, 56t, 60–61, endpapers.

Cover Credits

Air Portraits BCtl. Australian Picture Library Bg (ZEFA). Alan Ewart FCbl. Langdon G. Halls FCtr, BCbr. David Kirschner FCtl, FCc. NHPA FCcl (G. I. Bernard). John Richards FCcr. Steve Seymour FCbr.